THANK GOD IT'S SUNDAY!

Feb 3. 04

To ElFredia

From: Paul Miller

May health &
Wealth Be
Yours!

Bernard Smalls has done it!

In T.G.I Sunday he takes deep concepts of service and spirituality and makes them light-hearted and humorous. If you have been bored and confused with books on customer service, you must read this COMPELLING PARABLE BASED ON A TRUE STORY OF THREE SIMPLE PRINCIPLES THAT WILL CHANGE YOUR LIFE BY IMPROVING YOUR SERVE!

T. G. I.

Sunday
The Gospel of Customer Service

The Great Awakening of
Customer Retention!

General market research reveals that it costs six times as much to get new customers as it does to retain old ones!

O. Bernard Smalls
Corporate Trainer

THANK GOD IT'S SUNDAY!

◆

The Gospel of Customer Service

O. Bernard Smalls

iUniverse, Inc.
New York Lincoln Shanghai

THANK GOD IT'S SUNDAY!
The Gospel of Customer Service

iUniverse, Inc.

For information address:
iUniverse, Inc.
2021 Pine Lake Road, Suite 100
Lincoln, NE 68512
www.iuniverse.com

ISBN: 0-595-29606-8

Printed in the United States of America

DEDICATED TO:

Dr. Ken and Margie Blanchard
Thanks Ken and Margie for showing so many of us the way. Your teachings and
examples have had a tremendous and positive impact on my life. The two weeks I
spent in your home were certainly life changing. You are both definitely loving teach-
ers of simple truths. This book could not exist without your generous spirits.

Contents

TGIS-DAY CHEERS!
ACKNOWLEDGEMENTS

Karen Smalls—my wife, my clover and my lover!
Alexia Smalls—my ten-year old daughter for title cover design and creative suggestions
Travian, Terrence, and Aaron—my three sons—☺
Ken & Margie Blanchard—for being pioneers and great examples of excellence
Peter J. Daniels—for the wake up call to wealth and greatness
Jerome Smalls and Linda Taylor—for opening the door of opportunity
John Williams—for allowing me to dance with the Giants!
Shawn Esfahani—for believing in me!
Rusty Gentry—my brother...
Sara Caverhill—for your optimism and faith in my training potential
Bishop Eddie Long—for loading my spiritual entrepreneurial shotgun!
Darwin Ashley—for being a great servant and my main man!
Gwen Edwards—for editing assistance on the original book
Nicole Harris—for showing up at a key time
Carol Harris—for your feedback and grammatical help
The Southeast Automotive Group Team Members—you are the greatest!
Susan Massey—for your editorial eye, and for being "Susan"—you are the best!
The Founding Concepts Faith family—thanks for your support.
The Lord Jesus Christ!—My Best Friend!

INTRODUCTION

During my years as Corporate Trainer for Toyota Mall, one of the fastest growing Toyota franchises in history, I experienced a lot of fun and fulfillment as I endeavored to teach hundreds of employees the concepts of Raving Fan customer service. My role was to improve the human performance systems of the organization in the areas of sales excellence and customer service. I quickly found that clichés did not work! What I needed to produce was bottom line, measurable results.

Owner John Williams, before opening Toyota Mall, had for many successful years been the General Manager of Southeast Toyota. Southeast Toyota is the largest Toyota distributorship in the world. One of John's favorite words is *execution!* John is a passionate outcome oriented visionary. Through effectively implementing simple raving fan customer service principles, **we made history** by being the first Toyota dealership in the history of the world to win all Toyota performance excellence awards in the first year of business, including the prestigious President's Award. A focus on outstanding customer service made the difference. This book is designed to bring the power of timeless truths into your practical everyday work life to help you do exploits in the marketplace!

The customer service crisis of the 21st century demands serving at a higher level. As you read this parable, based on a true account of success through the gospel of customer service, I believe that you will see that the spiritual and the practical can work together to produce a level of service that will amaze the world.

The Gospel of Customer Service is good news and the three spiritual principles will truly help you build lasting relationships with the people you serve!

O. Bernard Smalls
Suwanee, Georgia
Spring 2003

1

"THANK GOD IT'S SUNDAY!"

This book is a journey into the potential for greatness in you! Yes, you have the potential for greatness. I firmly believe that deep within each human being is the question, "What makes the great, great?" As you read this book I believe that you will discover that the real key to true greatness is to be of service to others. The setting I have created for this book is an automobile dealership that is out of this world. Even if you are not in the car business the principles of service will change your life if you will read, digest and apply the three spiritual principles. If you are in the automobile industry, get ready for an exciting journey of how to serve with excellence, have fun and fulfillment and, if you want, make big bucks.

No matter who you are, if you are breathing you are in customer service in one way or another because you are in the people business. You can be a shining star if you learn how to serve others with excellence. You need to read it and reap the life changing benefits. I have lived it! As they say been there, done that!

By the way, this book really has nothing to do with religion, as most people understand religion. It's really about the true religion of being kind to others and serving them with excellence in every way whether at home, work, the market-place, the church, the synagogue or even in the world of entertainment. So relax! If you are a coffee drinker, we could be of kindred spirits. Great coffee and this book are extremely compatible. ☺

Read and enjoy while I introduce you to some everyday people and profound concepts that will bring to you true wealth and greatness through service. In this book I want you to open your imagination while I introduce you to four shining stars: Oscar, Tom, George, and Sally.

But first…guess what day it is! It's Sunday, let's go with Joe and Zack on a journey…

...IT'S SUNDAY!

Joseph Simple and his friend Zack Billiard pulled up in Joe's new BMW to the contemporary corporate headquarters building to see a mass of excited people passing through the large beautiful entry into the butterfly shaped pavilion. Some were wearing jeans, and some wore shorts. Others were conservatively casual. They were young, old, black, white, Asian, Hispanic, you name it. The one constant that captured Joe's attention was the enthusiasm they all seemed to have. After they were seated, the band started playing some upbeat contemporary music and Joe leaned over and said to his friend Zack, "This is different." Zack just looked at him with a big smile and said, "Thanks for coming with me today Joe."

They sang three songs along with the band and then the Pastor came to the pulpit, comfortably but well dressed in a dark blue sports coat with a black turtleneck and sat down. After a young, attractive teenaged soloist had finished her song, the Pastor stood up and said to the congregation "Good morning and welcome to our service!"

The minister then said to the congregation, "Now let's all say **THANK GOD IT'S SUNDAY!**" After this affirmation you could hear light laughter and enthusiastic chuckles ignite throughout the beautiful non-religious Church auditorium. People obviously felt good about being there.

The Pastor then proclaimed, "Today's sermon is entitled The Gospel of Customer Service. My thesis is the call to wealth. As he opened his Bible he asked the crowd, "Did you know that the word gospel literally means good news or a good message? The good news is that excellent customer service is not just for Sunday. It's for everyday!

A message on customer service may seem like a strange title for a Sunday morning Church service, but remember the good news is not just for Sunday. I preach a positive theology because people don't need to hear how bad they are; they need to hear how good God is. They need to hear good news. A part of that good news is financial prosperity and greatness for those who learn how to serve others with excellence.

Many people don't understand the importance of the practical issue of service. I believe that *excellent service* is directly linked to the financial prosperity of an organization or a business. Financial prosperity in an organization is in direct proportion to how it takes care of customers, partners, members, and markets. As my good friend Ken Blanchard puts it "Profit is the applause we get for taking care of our customers."

God gives us the power to create wealth. Even Socrates said:

> *"Wealth does not bring goodness, but goodness brings wealth and every other blessing, both to the individual and the state".*
> —Socrates

Wealth can be enjoyed by understanding this practical and spiritual message of making a 100% commitment to the simple, yet profound, concept of excellent customer service!"

The Minister continued, "Nordstrom became a favorite shopping spot while I lived in the Northwest. At one time, for approximately five years straight, I visited Nordstrom at least once a week to buy a shirt, a tie, or just to get a fresh hot cup of Seattle's Best Coffee. John W. Nordstrom started his business in the early 1900's with a *vision* of outstanding customer service that has continued to grow for more than a century."

The Pastor went on to say, "I was reading a book entitled Fabled Service by Betsy Sanders recently that explained the gospel according to Nordstrom by the following phrase: **"This is what we are here for; to serve and be kind!"**

Reportedly, one delighted customer went so far as to stipulate in her will that her ashes be scattered at Nordstrom. "That way", she said, "I am certain my chil-

dren will visit me often." The minister told the congregation the challenge to be of service or to be extraordinarily kind brings out the best in everybody!

"In my estimation, Nordstrom is certainly a great customer service organization. How many of you have shopped Nordstrom?" Many hands went up. Several people leaned over to the person seated next to them and whispered the impact Nordstrom had on them. Nordstrom is committed to 100% guaranteed customer satisfaction.

In my years as a corporate trainer, I found that all great organizations have a certain mind-set about service. Their central focus is always the customer. I believe that it's high time that we learn the good virtues from the great organizations and then take it to another level through God's great love for humanity.

This may be challenging for "religious" folks but God said in Luke 16: 8, "the children of this world are in their generation wiser than the children of light." Why did God say they are wiser? When it comes to dealing in the everyday practical affairs of business and money making, the children of this age are often wiser than the average religious Joe. The Pastor proclaimed, "The Gospel of Customer Service is simply wisdom and common sense. However, Zig Ziglar says, "Common sense is not always common practice!"

I know it's obvious that I am really passionate about customer service. If you were to take a knife and cut me open, customer service excellence would bleed out of me. (But don't try it. I don't like the sight of blood).

The Pastor asked, "Does God know anything about service?" A handsome, heavy set, well-dressed, black gentleman in the normally calm auditorium shouted, **"Amen bro!"**

Let me use a theological phrase for emphasis. Many customer service representatives need to repent and believe the Gospel of Customer Service. We have all seen customer endearing signs at businesses such as:

- MANAGEMENT RESERVES THE RIGHT TO REFUSE SERVICE TO ANYBODY!

- NO CHANGES OR SUBSTITUTIONS ALLOWED!

- ALL SALES ARE FINAL!

Remember we are talking about the Gospel (good news) of Customer Service, not calling down fire and brimstone on people that bring us complaints.

There are three major factors or principles that, when understood and properly implemented, make an organization *excellent* in customer service. You could call these the triple bottom line to super customer service. **The three spiritual principles are:**

1. **Meaningful Service Vision**

2. **Customer Oriented People**

3. **Customer Friendly Systems**

The minister summarized and concluded his sermon by saying, "The good news is that we all can improve on our customer service and be better family members, citizens, and have a positive affect in our world. A customer is simply anyone that depends on you to get a need met. The Gospel of Customer Service is great because it fulfils the golden rule: Do unto others as you would have them do unto you!

2

JAVA TIME

Joe Simple, formerly a successful C.T.O. (chief technology officer), had been invited to Church to hear the Pastor's sermon on The Gospel of Customer Service by Zack, a former co-worker. After Church, they stopped by the local Starbucks to have a couple of flavored lattes. As they sat and sipped the gourmet coffee, Aretha Franklin's R.E.S.P.E.C.T. played in the background and people were lined at the counter awaiting their java fixes.

Zack asked Joe, "Well, did you enjoy the service?" Joe said, "Funny that you should ask. I know I have been a little quiet, but it's because I have been pondering the whole experience. To say the least, it was different. I was raised Episcopalian and was not quite prepared for all of the contemporary stuff and the message on wealth in Church. The whole thing just did not seem religious enough for me. The Pastor didn't even wear a tie or a robe and that blew me away. Plus, I had always been taught in Church that poverty was a virtue. It all sounded good, but I have always been warned to look out for things that sound too good to be true. The people were all very nice, and everything was excellent, especially the music. In fact, I felt a little guilty for enjoying the rhythm section of the band. I expected a choir with a grand piano and not the *Atlanta Rhythm Section.*

"Yet I must say there were a lot of young and elderly people there that seemed to be getting a lot out of this non-religious approach to Church. I am still weighing the whole experience." Zack saw that this was no time to put the pressure on. Joe still needed time to sort it all out.

Zack simply replied, "Interesting comments. Thanks for the feedback. Do you want another shot of java, Joe?" Joe yelled to the girl behind the counter to bring two more rounds of the same. The young lady smiled and enthusiastically replied, "*My pleasure!*"

3

MONDAY, MONDAY...!

It's Monday morning and Joe Simple woke up at 4: 00 AM in a cold sweat. He was worried about how he would maintain his standard of living. The 9/11 terrorist attacks and the subsequent lay-offs at "Quality Plus," an Atlanta based technology communications firm, had put him in a challenging financial position after losing his six figure income, benefits, and position as a Chief Technology Officer.

As he pondered his situation, his mind went back to the Pastor's sermon, especially the part about the call to wealth. Joe had visited the church to repay a favor to Zack. Zack knew Joe's concerns about his financial future since the lay-off and thought the minister's message could be his answer. Joe had been a hit and miss church go-er, and not quite what you would call a fan of spiritual things. He had a casual approach to religion and believed it was a personal issue and not to be discussed in public. He had a real distaste for anything that resembled being a religious fanatic, Bible thumper, or a Jesus freak.

As Joe lay in the bed this Monday morning, he thought deeply on the sermon. It seemed that the Pastor's words just kept ringing in his heart. He looked over at his wife who was sound asleep and decided to get up and brew some fresh coffee. While having a hot cup of Starbuck's coffee, he picked up and started looking through the local paper. As he glanced through the want ads, he saw an ad in the sales section that said:

"OPPORTUNITY FOR BIG BUCKS"
50–90K Annually
Please call Oscar at
EXCELLENT WAY AUTOMOTIVE GROUP
770.555.1234

Joe looked at the pay and thought, "That's too good to be true! Nobody can possibly make that kind of money selling cars." Joe had seen the movies SUCKERS and USED CARS and thought they depicted the totality of the car sales profession. He thought they were all car dogs! He thought to himself, "The reputation of a car salesman is not the image I want. They are all scumbags. How can I go from being a Chief Technology Officer to being car salesmen? That would be like selling your soul to the devil. They are like liars that create more and more lies everyday to rip off innocent people. The scum of the earth..." Then Joe caught himself and said, "Man, you are getting negative. The lay-off and consequent financial situation is getting to you mentally and emotionally. I guess all car salesmen are not car dogs." He jotted the number in his day-timer and continued to look for I.T. jobs.

Joe saw that the section on I.T. positions had shrunk to just a few lines. And each one he called had filled the position and was still receiving an average of 7,500 resumes a day by monster.com, the mail, and other sources. He kept looking at job ads the rest of the morning. At noon, in desperation, looking at his dwindling savings account, he decided he would call the number of the car dealership after lunch.

Joe had worked part-time in car sales for a car dealership, as he did his undergrad studies at Atlanta University and completing his MBA at Georgia Business Technology Institute. It was okay for a college job, but he never thought he would end up in the car business again. Besides, he was looking into the New Age Religion seeking to find his spiritual footing in life and realized that his experience in the auto business was not the image he had of being a good, ethical, peaceful person. And, as far as morality and quality of life were concerned, well…the movies SUCKERS and USED CARS just kept running through his mind. I can't do this, he thought as he looked at the OPPORTUNITY FOR BIG BUCKS ad, again. As he looked this time he noticed a small fish at the bottom of the ad. *Could these guys that own this business be religious or Christians. That could be great!* Immediately, he became doubtful. "Yeah, I bet that fish is a front. They are probably just a group of greedy crooks." Joe kept looking in the ads only to find that lucrative I.T. jobs were few and far between since the 9/11 attacks. "What am I going to do?" he thought. "I just can't bow that low to being a car salesman."

"The image of the fat, fast talking, lying, cigarette smoking car salesperson is just not who I am. I'll just wait it out. I bet we will catch that stupid Ben Ladin and all of the terrorism stuff will blow over, so that once again we can enjoy the good old "I.T. days". I just can't call that dealership." He went on-line, only to find more of the same thing: layoffs, downsizing, closures, and unemployment rates increasing. He said, "I still have some savings and 401K money. I'll just tough it out."

4

CRUNCH TIME

Six months later, Joe had called every I.T. ad, followed every lead, and networked every contact he could find to no avail. Savings were dwindling and desperation was setting in. Things were only getting worse in the once money-spinning I.T. industry. You could say the game had changed after 9/11. He went back to the drawer that he had thrown the EXCELLENT WAY AUTOMOTIVE GROUP ad, only to find the OPPORTUNITY FOR BIG BUCKS caption staring him in the face. He thought, "Even if this is a hoax; it's crunch time. I am ready to give it a try to generate some cash flow." He humorously thought, "At least it would be better than making a *will work for food* sign."

He called the dealership and was amazed at how pleasant, cheerful, and professional the receptionist was. She answered, "It's a Great Day at Excellent Way! How can I serve you?" Joe said, "Wow, what a greeting. I am calling about the ad in the paper for salespersons." The receptionist said, "Great, our sales people are some of my favorite people in the world. I'll connect you to Mr. Oscar Paywell's office. He does the interviewing and hiring." Oscar's administrative assistant thanked Joe for calling and told him how business was booming and they needed more sales professionals. Joe could hardly believe business could be so great for Excellent Way while the I.T. field is experiencing such a slump. Joe asked, "How could business possibly be booming?" The assistant replied, "Mr. Simple, our business is always good due to our strong customer service positioning. We believe that if you take care of customers in the good times they will honor you with their patronage during the lean times. In addition to this, interest rates are at an all time low since the terrorist attacks so you could say it is a buyer's market. Finally, this area is the fastest growing area of the country, second only to Vegas." Joe thought, "ah-ha. Even Vegas might not be a bad idea right now."

He set up an appointment for an interview with Oscar for Thursday of the same week. On Thursday morning, Joe jumped into one of his best conservative corporate suits with a white shirt and tie, hopped into his BMW and headed to EXCELLENT WAY to meet Oscar.

5

A GREAT DAY AT EXCELLENT WAY!

As Joe pulled up to the gate of the dealership he was shocked to see that a valet came literally running to his car saying, "It's a great day at EXCELLENT WAY. Thanks for visiting us, how can we serve you?" Joe asked, "What's up with the security gate and the valet service? Is this the CHEESECAKE FACTORY or a car dealership?" The valet replied, "Great sense of humor sir. We are committed to the Gospel of Customer Service here. Our mission statement is **TO SERVE THE MORE EXCELLENT WAY.** We do our best to make sure our customers have a great experience. And, even if they don't buy an automobile, we want to help brighten their day by the EXCELLENT WAY experience." While the valet was still talking, a luxury golf cart came zooming around the corner. The driver, a very pleasant Haitian man, greeted and picked up Joe and took him to the foyer of the executive offices. Joe tried to give the driver a tip but the driver said, "No thank you, Sir. We are here to give to, and not take from, our guests. Enjoy your day at EXCELLENT WAY! Here is my card with my two way radio number and here is a radio for you. If you need me to take you anywhere on the grounds feel free to page me or press 000 for the operator and she would be glad to page me." Joe was stunned and walked away shaking his head. As he walked up to the entry of the foyer, the thought hit him. "Wow, and I'm just here for an interview, I wonder how they treat their customers?"

As he walked up to the door he could not help but notice how excellent and beautiful everything was. The signs were all brightly painted and strategically placed to give the customers directions. The lawn and flowers were absolutely immaculate. All of the people were especially nice, including the lawn crew and porters. He immediately noticed that there were no eardrum piercing pages from the sales desk for people out on the lot. Instead, they all had two-way radios. Even the lot attendants and the lawn crew communicated with two-way radios.

His image of the car business was gradually changing. Could this be real or is it just a front to get people in? "I know the drill", Joe thought. "There is always a hook in the bait. This is probably just a part of their *Bait and Switch* tactic. You know, fatten them up for the kill."

Joe walked up to the automatic sliding doors and was met by a lovely, pleasant female greeter who said, "IT'S A GREAT DAY AT EXCELLENT WAY! How can I serve you?" "I'm here to see Oscar Paywell for an interview." "Great I will page him. Please have a seat sir. Mr. Paywell will be with you shortly." Joe sat in the huge, comfortable, all leather chair near the greeter's station looking at all of the awards that EXCELLENT WAY had earned, enjoying the smooth jazz and the beautiful art work. "Oscar is just wrapping up a meeting Mr. Simple. Would you like a beverage while you wait?" Joe said, "I'll take a diet coke please." The greeter said, "Coming right up!" as she picked up the phone to contact the dealership's in-house deli. The waiter from the deli came dressed in a tux, with a large cup of ice and two diet cokes with lemon. Joe said, "Wow, is this the Ritz Carlton?" The waiter smiled and said, "We want to make it a GREAT DAY at EXCELLENT WAY for all of our guests." Joe thought, "This all looks good on the front, but I bet there's a snake in the bushes somewhere, and I'll find it. Car dealerships are all about CASH. When I was working part-time in a dealership in college, my sales manager continually said CASH IS KING! You know, fatten them up and put the knife in them."

While Joe waited he thought, "I'll bet the restrooms are not as excellent. I was told in a training class that the condition of the restrooms tells the truth about the business."

As Joe walked on the luxurious wood floors in the hallway to go to the restrooms, he was astonished by the responsiveness of all of the support staff and sales personnel, who were all excellently dressed in blue and gold. He had always been taught that car sales people are just sales dogs who are only friendly to people who put cash in their pockets.

As Joe approached the restroom door, he smiled and thought, "Now is the moment of truth." As he touched the door, it opened electronically and he immediately heard the classical music and smelled the strawberry air freshener that was being sprayed in a mist through ceiling ducts. The beautiful oak trimming and soft lighting made it a rich place to experience. An attendant dressed in blue and gold was stationed in the men's room to provide assistance to any guest in need. The attendant, a handsome middle-aged man said, "IT'S A GREAT DAY AT EXCELLENT WAY! Thanks for visiting us." Joe walked up to the sink to freshen up and noticed every kind of hygiene item you would need or desire including mouthwash, disposable toothbrushes, and toothpaste. There were also small samples of men's cologne for a little touch up. He washed his hands and looked for the disposable towels. He was surprised that the counter was stacked with real cloth towels and a large beautiful wicker basket near by to toss the used ones. The sign above the towels with the days' date that said, "EXCELLENT WAY THOUGHT FOR THE DAY: Only the Best for Our Guests and You Are the Best!" Joe walked out of the rest room literally scratching and shaking his head.

As soon as Joe returned to his diet coke and took a seat in the large comfortable leather chair, Oscar Paywell came out with a bounce in his steps, also conservatively but excellently dressed in blue and gold with a cheerful smile and said, "You must be Mr. Simple. Thanks for coming in today. IT'S A GREAT DAY AT EXCELLENT WAY! I'm Oscar Paywell, the Apostle of Customer Service and the C.E.O. of Excellent Way Automotive Group." Joe said, "I guess so!" as he nearly choked. Joe was a little shocked by Oscar's boldness to identify himself as an Apostle. Oscar said, "I have been looking forward to meeting you. Let's go to my office."

Oscar had the greeter page a waiter from the deli to bring Joe's partially finished diet coke, along with a fresh drink, and some extra lemons to his office. Joe said, "Mr. Paywell, before we get started I want to ask you something." "Go right ahead", said Oscar. "But please call me Oscar." Joe said, "I know this may sound kind of dumb, but why am I in the executive offices for an interview to be a sales person?" Oscar said, "It's not a dumb question at all. I get it all the time. The answer is simple. We believe in delivering outstanding customer service to *every* guest. You are a guest Joe. Everyone that drives or walks onto this property is treated like a guest, a king or a queen. Besides that, I am the primary owner and I like to hand pick my sales consultants because they represent me as they interact with our customers. So, I invite them into my world so they can see what the heart and the head of our business is like, instead of into some dingy interview room. First, we believe in our people. We like to make people feel special and there is nothing special in a grimy interview or training room. We also understand the power of first impressions. In fact, take a look at this." He pointed to a beautifully framed motivational quote that said *You Never Get a Second Chance to Make a First Impression.* "By the way, that was a gift from my good friend Peter J. Daniels who is an extremely successful Australian Spiritual Entrepreneur." The thought Spiritual Entrepreneur lingered in Joe's mind during the rest of the interview and during the tour of the facilities. It reminded him of the concepts he heard in the sermon when he visited Zack's Church several months earlier.

Joe followed Oscar past his executive desk and they went and sat at a handsome round oak table in the south end of his office. He noticed a beautiful poster that said:

"Commitment to Excellence"

"The quality of a man's life will be in direct proportion to his commitment to excellence, no matter what his chosen field of endeavor is."
— Vince Lombardi

Oscar said, "Thanks for coming in for an interview Joe. Feel free to help yourself to the cookies and finger food." After a little more small talk and rapport building, Oscar got right down to business. "Joe, I am a *Spiritual Entrepreneur*. That is why I humorously introduced myself as the Apostle of Customer Service." Joe said, "You sure did get my attention with that greeting. What does this spiritual stuff have to do with business and customer service?"

Oscar said, "Let me explain. I operate my store by practical and spiritual principles. You don't have to be religious to work here, but we look for people with great hearts, hearts of customer service.

I believe that as a Spiritual Entrepreneur I am called to wealth, and I use that wealth to take care of my family, serve humanity, and to be a blessing to those in need." Joe thought, "This stuff sounds familiar." But, he kept silent about his visit to his friend's church.

Oscar continued, "If this sounds good to you so far let me carry on. If not, we can terminate the interview and part as friends." Joe said, "Oh no, Mr. Paywell. I find this interesting. It reminds me of a Church I attended a few months ago." Oscar said, "Joe call me Oscar, please. Don't make me feel old. Here is some information from Fred Wiersema's awesome book *Customer Service* based on research about American Businesses:

- More than half of all businesses in the U.S. are service related, and those who perform best will dominate the market in the coming years.

- Men, women and children are no longer subject to the whims of product manufacturers.

- Companies today must provide quality products at a reasonable price *just to stay in business.* To thrive, companies must treat customers well.

- Few organizations, if any, can thrive today without repeat business. That means that any organization that wants to survive must not only attract new customers, but must also keep existing ones excited.

Oscar smiled and said softly, "Joe, Spiritual Entrepreneurs are really in the life changing business. We create wealth and make money to help others! Because of this we take business very seriously. Jesus, the greatest servant of all time said in John 2: 49…"I must be about my Father's business…What do you think of all this?"

Joe responded, "Well, I am a relatively good person, but not a religious person per se. I used to attend the Episcopalian Church regularly in New Jersey. But, since moving to Atlanta, I have let it slip. But you know, Oscar, I have been thinking about my spiritual journey a lot lately. I even went to this contemporary Church with a friend recently, but I don't want to be a Jesus freak. I just want to enjoy peace of mind and prosperity for my family."

Oscar said, "I like what I'm feeling Joe. This could be the place for you. But let me ask you some very important questions." Oscar pulled out a formal interview sheet and asked Joe twelve questions that were designed to find out his motivation, his energy and his ethics. Joe responded with sweaty palms and wondered if he was answering right. Not to speak of his concern with the fact that he may not have been spiritual enough to work for a *Spiritual Entrepreneur*. After the questions were all answered, Oscar pulled out his reading glasses and went over Joe's responses with a fine tooth comb.

After a brief period of silent reflection Oscar said, "I like what I am sensing. How is the diet coke holding out? Do you need another beverage?" "No thanks. One more and I'll float away." Oscar said, "Please follow me." He led Joe to a computer to take a personality test. "Please sit at this terminal and complete the AVA test." Joe felt the leather arms on the chair at the computer terminal and said, "That's good stuff." Oscar said, "Only the Best for Our Guests!" Joe sat in the comfortable leather chair then asked, "Oscar, what in the world is an AVA test? I have taken hundreds of tests on the job and in the many training programs that Quality Plus required that I attend to keep my I.T. certifications, but never an AVA." "It's a test to show us your sales personality tendencies, your assertiveness and your maturity. AVA is an acronym for ACTIVITY VECTOR ANALYSIS." Oscar continued, "I am a trained Executive AVA Analyst. I will go over the numbers when you are through. When the test is over, just press the blue button on the keyboard and I'll be right there." After the test, Oscar concluded the formal interview and let Joe know that he would be in contact as soon as the results from the standard pre-employment screens were in.

Joe couldn't help but notice the plaque over Oscar's door as they were both walking out. It said:

"Fulfilled, happy customers are the lifeblood of a business".
—Ritz Carlton

Oscar escorted Joe to the main exit door and beeped the porter on the NEX-TEL to bring Joe's car up to the door. Joe said, "Wow, the place is certainly world class." Oscar said, "Thanks Joe. By the way, here's my card."

As Joe was leaving the interview, he thought, "This is interesting. This guy seems to be very spiritual, yet very practical when it comes to business, especially customer service. And, if the service to customers is anyway near how I was treated today, I want this job. I never thought anything good could come out of a car dealership, but I was wrong. I think this guy is the real deal." Joe left the interview and jumped into his BMW. He tried again to give the porter a tip. The guy refused and said with a smile, "I hope you enjoyed your brief stay at EXCEL-LENT WAY." Joe said, "You folks are almost poetic, and the service is first class." The young man said, "Thanks Mr. Simple" great service is our pleasure." He jumped in, turned on the air and headed straight for the local Starbucks to have his favorite drink, a Venti sugar-free vanilla latte.

6

THE WAITING GAME!

The following morning, Joe sat in his kitchen having coffee with his lovely wife. He was watching CNN, listening to world events when he just out of the blue said, "I want it!" His wife asked, "You want what?" "I'm sorry honey. I just have my fingers crossed anxiously, hoping I get the job at EXCELLENT WAY." He then sighed doubtfully, "I bet they won't call me. I'm such a heathen they will probably hire some religious fanatic. But Oscar, the owner, did say at one point in the interview *I like what I'm sensing.*" His wife responded, "Time will tell honey. Whether you get the job or not you are still my hero. Joe, do you want some more coffee?" "Yeah, a refill would be fine." Joe said to his wife, "You sure are in a serving mood lately, what's gotten into you?"

At 10:00 AM sharp the phone started to ring. Joe's wife looked at the caller I.D. and said, "Honey, honey! It's a call from EXCELLENT WAY!" Joe ran across the room and grabbed the phone nearly knocking her over. "Joe Simple speaking!" "Hi Joe. This is Oscar Paywell at EXCELLENT WAY Automotive Group. Joe, this morning while I was praying, I got a real peace about bringing you into the company. We meet every morning at 6: 00 AM to pray for our families and the business. After praying over those applicants, we agreed that you should come and work on our sales team." Joe was excited and said, "Great! I'll take it. When do you want me there? Yesterday I bet." Oscar said, "No. Just enjoy the weekend and we would like to see you Monday morning at 9: 00 for orientation and customer service training."

Joe got off the phone and said, "Hallelujah!" as he did a dance. He said, "Honey, I got it!" "Great", said his wife. "I prayed yesterday with that Smalley guy on TV for peace and prosperity for our marriage and family." Joe said, "Whatever you did it worked. Let's go celebrate. How about a Starbuck's Venti Latte?" "Let's go!" As they were driving, Joe started to wonder about the *spiritual implication* of all that was happening. First he thought, "I'm really blessed to get this job." Then he thought, "Am I becoming a Jesus freak? Better slow down."

He even had a concern about whether he was getting into a cult. He thought, "What if this Oscar guy is some Jim Jones?" He laughed at himself as he thought, "I surely won't be drinking any Kool-Aid!" Through it all, he was excited about the income opportunity for big bucks and thought, "Everyone there was so nice. It surely can't be a cult!" His wife said, "Honey! You just passed Starbucks." Joe said, "I'm sorry. I was in another world for a moment," as he wheeled his stylish BMW around to head to Starbucks.

7

TRAINING DAY—ONE

◆

The More Excellent Way

Joe showed up on Monday morning at 8:30 sharp for the EXCELLENT WAY orientation and customer service training. He thought it strange that a car dealership would put its sales people through customer service training before teaching them anything about selling cars. Oscar told him that customer service training was first and foremost to be followed by Beware of Car Dawgs—The Twelve Fundamentals to a Sale. Oscar said, "My vision is service first, sale second." Joe thought the training concept was impressive and interesting.

As he walked into the beautifully decorated training room, his ears were filled with the wonderful sound of smooth jazz. The music was piped through the high quality stereo speakers. He also noticed the wonderful breakfast spread, the motivational pictures on the wall, and the gigantic screen for a power point presentation and four flip charts strategically placed. Joe thought to himself, "Everything here is so first class." He said to one of the waiters assigned to keep the breakfast fresh and serve the trainees, "This sure is first class for a car dealership." The waiter smiled and said, "Thank you Mr. Simple. First class service is our pleasure." Since Joe was plenty early, he got a plate of breakfast goodies and found the table with his name typed on the blue and gold nameplate, sat down and started reading the orientation materials that were on the tables in front of his nameplate. He reflected on the title, The Gospel of Customer Service. For a moment, he thought it sounded kind of religious, but everything seemed heavenly anyway. Let's get it on…

Oscar Paywell came in and greeted the class with an enthusiastic good morning and said, "You are God's best and we are thrilled to have you as a part of our team. How many of you enjoyed the breakfast?" Joe said, "It was awesome! I'm still licking my chops." "Great. Our chefs prepared a good old-fashion breakfast especially for you. Tomorrow we will have the traditional continental breakfast. But, today we wanted to give you a finger-licking treat to show our appreciation for becoming a team member."

While Oscar was talking, two well-groomed men and a tall attractive woman came in and sat in the rear of the training room. Oscar welcomed them and told the group that he had invited three of the EXCELLENT WAY shinning stars to meet with the new trainees. As soon as Oscar said shining stars, Earth, Wind and Fire was piped through the training room sound system performing You Are a Shining Star. All of the trainees started to clap or whistle. "You will spend more time with them later in the training process. The first star I want you to meet is from our sales department and she is Sally Sellers." Sally just waved as they gave her a round of applause.

"The next gentleman is Tom Treadwell from the service department." The class again started to applaud. "Last but not least, from our parts department is George Goodwrench." The class once again started to applaud. Oscar complimented the class for being so Gung Ho in cheering others on. Oscar thanked the three service stars for coming in and told them they could return to their departments.

"You will learn some foundational concepts of the Gospel of Customer Service that could change your entire life during the next three days. If you buy into these principles of Customer Service, we will place you in the sales training class. If you don't, we simply part company in peace. Is that fair? We want people that buy into our customer service culture more than we want sales people that can sell a lot of cars. Our commitment to excellence has caused us to make a decision not to have a sales staff of car dogs. We want people that will put our customers first, and serve like they would want to be served if they were purchasing an automobile. Some of the local dealerships have even made fun of how they abuse customers by lying about things like trade in value, the interest rate, and the price of the vehicle—then saying THE DEVIL MADE ME DO IT! Hah, hah! Well, at EXCELLENT WAY, the devil isn't making us do anything! We are here to serve our guests with excellence."

THE GREAT AWAKENING

Oscar continued, "Let's talk about The Great Awakening—Customer Retention Management.

We are committed to making a difference by taking care of our customers. We call it the Gospel of Customer Service! Take a look at the screen." The first power point heading said: THE GREAT AWAKENING OF THE 21ST CENTURY: THE C.R.M. WAVE!

Oscar explained, "Customer Retention Management has become the great awakening of the 21st century. Smart business owners have awakened to know that it costs six times as much to gain new customers as it costs to retain old ones. What is your attitude about retaining customers?"

Here are some statistics to consider:

Why Businesses Lose Customers

- 1% Died

- 3% Moved Away

- 5% Influenced by Friends

- 9% Lured Away by Competition

- 14% Dissatisfied with Products

- 68% Turned Away by an Attitude of Indifference on the part of a Company Employee

---

Oscar continued with an emphasis on service by saying, "Customers desire delightful service. What makes service delightful? Here are some one-word answers: Unexpected, Undeserved, and Unnecessary! These are service values that let the customer know the organization really cares! The Gospel of Customer Service is quite simply ordinary people doing ordinary things extraordinarily well!"

Oscar's timer started to beep and he said, "It's break time, let's take 15 minutes, go outside and get some fresh air, a cappuccino from the dealership's deli downstairs or just stay here in the training room and enjoy the music."

After the break, Oscar welcomed the class back. "The Gospel of Customer Service guarantees increase in any business, but first we must understand the nature of the customer".

Oscar then walked briskly across the room, smiled at the group and flipped the sheet on a large flipchart and said, "Let's get some understanding of who our customer is.

WHO IS MY CUSTOMER?

- The lawyer calls him a CLIENT.
- The doctor calls him a PATIENT.
- The hotel calls him a GUEST.
- The editor calls him a SUBSCRIBER.
- The broadcaster calls him a LISTENER-VIEWER.
- The retailer calls him a SHOPPER.
- The educator calls him a STUDENT.
- The manufacturer calls him a DEALER.
- The politician calls him a VOTER.
- The banker calls him a DEPOSITOR/BORROWER.
- The sports promoter calls him a FAN.
- The railroad executive calls him a PASSENGER.
- The minister calls him a MEMBER.

The customer is the person that comes to us for products, service, or solutions. The customer is the reason for the organization's existence!

We are here to serve. If you don't understand the concept of serving from the root, the nature, you will offer a surface type of serving. You only serve for what you can get out of it. Service is actually a spiritual concept. What Does It Mean To Serve?

> *"We are Ladies and Gentlemen*
> *Serving Ladies and Gentlemen"*
> **—The Ritz Carlton**

The Ritz Carlton is known for outstanding customer service. Oscar pointed to the poster that emphasized their motto of serving ladies and gentlemen. "Service can best be better understood by going back to the original Greek language. According to Strong's Exhaustive Concordance, here is the meaning of the word serve: Greek—douleuo; *to be a slave;* from doulos; *subjection* or *subservience* (volunteer or in-volunteer) Subservience: lit. (sub means below) to get below and serve. The Greek word for deacon—diakonos, literally means a servant."

After this in depth word study with the group, Oscar asked the group, "Do you need a break? I'm sure your brain needs it after that word study session." The group responded, "Keep on. This is interesting stuff." Oscar said, "Thanks for the compliment but we will take a break. I believe that the mind can endure no longer than the behind." ☺ After these training instructions, Oscar and the trainees took a break to get some fresh air and walk around the grounds. Several of the trainees went outside and walked across the lawn to gaze at the ducks in a beautiful man-made lake out front. While standing there, a flock of Canadian geese came in honking for a landing in a nearly perfect V-formation. Joe silently watched the geese and admired the beauty of this event, as he experienced an inward sensation, *wondering what this meant,* if anything particular.

8

DESTINED FOR GREATNESS

After the break Oscar said, "Welcome back! Now, let's get practical about the power of service to make you great." Joe raised his hand and asked, "How often do you folks see the geese land on the lake out front?" Oscar said, "Only occasionally. All of the team members love to see that. It reminds them of my Gung Ho workshop!" "Gung Ho?" asked Joe. "What is that?" Oscar said, "Go pick up Ken Blanchard's book that bears the name Gung Ho and come back and tell me."

Oscar asked the group if they knew they are destined for greatness. Joe asked, "How can you say that everyone is destined for greatness? I know that people like Michael Jordon, Tiger Woods, and Madonna were destined for greatness, but how do you know we are?" "It's real simple when you understand the rewards of true service."

Dr. Albert Schweitzer, missionary and former head of hospitals in Africa said, "There is no higher religion than human service. To work for the common good is the greatest religion!" The word religion has its root in a Latin word meaning to bind together. Service, of all human endeavors has the greatest power to bind our lives together, to make them whole, and to give them meaning. James, in the Bible said, "True religion is to serve!"

The long and short of it is: service is the key to greatness and we can all be of service so we can all be great.

> "The tragedy of mankind is not this or that calamity,
> But the waste of man's potential for greatness!"
> **—William E. Channing**

Your success in life or business will be in direct proportion to what you do after you do what is expected of you. This is called going the extra mile. Great service organizations like the Ritz Carlton Hotel have learned this concept. They have even developed a corporate university to ingrain the attitude of outstanding service into the culture. The Ritz Carlton has three simple steps of service. **The first** is a warm and sincere greeting. **The second** is to use the guests' name, if and when possible. Focus on anticipation and compliance with guests' needs. **The final step is** a fond farewell. Give them a warm goodbye and again, use their name, if and when possible. At this point, Oscar referred to the training manual and read, "Every part of the facility, every staff member, and every product or process that bears the organization's name, reflects the level of respect you have for service to your guests and team members. Service is the key to greatness!"

Oscar introduced this to the group and Joe said out loud, "Wow. That's first class. Customer service is challenging and exciting!" Oscar said, "Amen Joe!"

Service Makes the Great—Great!

Service
No one achieves greatness without first being of service.
Service is the essence of greatness.
All great men and women become great because they gave
Some talent or ability in service to others.
And, no matter how small our talent,
We, too, can contribute in some way to others.
We too can become great!

Oscar then walked over to the training rooms' stereo system and put in an upbeat CD and said, "Guess what gang? It's break time!"

CREATING RAVING FANS!

After the break Oscar began, "I am not a namedropper but I am a personal friend with Dr. Ken Blanchard, the author of the classic book Raving Fans, Revolutionary Customer Service. I spent two weeks in his home by his personal invitation. That was one of the greatest experiences of my life. Ken and Margie are *real* people. Ken has said it well. *"The most important product in every business is customer service. People remember great service, and unfortunately they remember poor service even more."* Customer service is just as much a part of business as the product being sold."

The golden rule for every business is simple: **"Put yourself in the customer's place."**

Remember, excellent service consists of ordinary people doing ordinary things in extraordinary ways! It takes an instant to stop doing the less than excellent thing and a lifetime of practice to maintain doing the excellent…it is in practicing excellence in the small things that you prepare yourself to handle the major things with quality!

Now take a look at your training manuals. The page said Excellence in Service. The apostle of customer service explained that an organization's ability to maintain a reputation for high levels of service excellence is the key to its continued prosperity and success! He then pointed to the next power-point screen:

> "No matter what you do in our organization, your job title is "Problem Solver" and your job function is Customer Service Excellence."

Oscar asked the group, "Would service be as important a part of our economy tomorrow as it is today?" He answered for them, "**No**! IT WILL BE MORE IMPORTANT! By all indications the increasing shift from industrial America to service America, the demand for better and better services, and the increasing number of service jobs will make us all more service conscious. This will happen not only in America but also around the developed world. Every team member can aspire to higher standards of personal and corporate excellence! The major challenge in taking care of the customer is to never become so good at it that you can quit working on it. Being of service is a process that you will be perfecting for the rest of your life!"

Oscar then said to the trainees, "Being extraordinary demands commitment. You must become a student of service and read and observe all that you can about those who have based their lives on empowering others. You must also work on developing good service habits, one by one. You can start today. Pick the first less than excellent thing that you are going to stop doing—and the first excellent thing that you are going to start practicing. Track your new habits as they develop. Always give your best to the people you serve."

"Let's talk about taking it to the next level in customer service. The saying; "take it to the next level" has become a buzz phrase in the corporate world. C.E.O.s and corporate leadership are constantly challenging the executive and middle managers to develop strategies to take the organization to the next level. Often, the only reason to get to the next level is more money. The key to the next level is simple. It is making an absolute Commitment to Excellence as it pertains to customer service. Joe asked, "Are you saying that we should commit to excellent service because the customer is always right?" Oscar said, "Here is my take on that: RIGHT OR WRONG, THE CUSTOMER IS ALWAYS RIGHT!

We make the commitment because it is the right thing to do. We are committed to serve our customers with excellence, whether they are right or wrong in our thinking; THEY ARE ALWAYS RIGHT!"

When a customer enters my store, FORGET ME. He is king!"

As you commit to the Gospel of Customer Service, great things begin to happen. The Gospel of Customer Service means a no compromised commitment to serve our guests. To be the best we must offer the best possible service in our organizations.

Oscar took a pointer from the training table and pointed to the board and said, "Now we need to understand the Two Types of Customers: Internal and External Customers. Internal customers are anybody within the organization that depends on us for service. External customers are people who pay for our products and services. To deliver outstanding customer service we must understand the purpose of a business. The purpose of every business is to create and keep a customer. The best businesses take it to higher level by working on keeping internal and external customers."

MOMENTS OF TRUTH

...the truth shall make you free.

Oscar explained to the trainees that The Gospel of Customer Service demands that we understand the power of Moments of Truth. A moment of truth is any critical moment in customer service. The following phrase by Jan Carlzon, former president of Scandinavian Airlines, describes it well in his classic book entitled "Moments of Truth".

> *"A moment of truth is anytime a customer comes in contact with any aspect of our business, however remote, and has an opportunity to form an impression."*

So you must be aware of all the subtle opportunities you have everyday for impressing positively and all of the not so subtle opportunities you have for impressing negatively. Creating the right impression can be as simple as treating people the way you want to be treated. Or as difficult as treating them that way even though they are not cooperative. Every moment of truth is an opportunity to create a moment of magic! Physical moments of truth are your building, parking lot and sales materials. Personal moments of truth are telephone manners, warmth, and responsiveness to customer requests.

The rule with moments of truth is *Everything Counts!* Oscar concluded the session on Moments of Truth by explaining that most customers today experience many *moments of misery*. It is the norm to experience *moments of mediocrity*. The Gospel of Customer Service causes guests to experience *moments of magic*!

9

THE THREE SPIRITUAL PRINCIPLES

✦

A Meaningful Service Vision

After lunch, the class spent some time with Oscar, discussing what they had learned in the morning sessions and talking about how it applied in the work place at EXCELLENT WAY AUTOMOTIVE GROUP. After a vigorous discussion, Oscar said, "Now I know you have had a delicious lunch, but give me your best as we focus on the three core principles of how to operate in the Gospel of Customer Service. If you need to, get a cup of coffee and let's get the show on the road." Joe said, "I can handle a cup" and offered to *serve* the rest of the class. Oscar took him up on it and promptly thanked him for the piping hot shot of espresso from the dealership's coffee machine. "Ah! Coffee is good!" said Oscar.

We will now start to cover the first of the Three Simple Spiritual Principles for operating in the Gospel of Customer Service. Acting in sync with these concepts will release the awesome power of service excellence in our, or any, organization. They are:

1. *A Meaningful Service* **Vision**

2. *Customer Oriented* **People**

3. *Customer Friendly* **Systems**

Joe immediately thought, "That sounds familiar" as his mind raced back to the Church service at his friend Zack's positive upbeat Church.

Vision, People, and Systems…The trainer then had everyone repeat after him three times Vision, People, & Systems. He then said, "Remember repetition is the mother of skill and the seed of learning!"

Where there is no vision, the people perish…

Now that we have a basic philosophy of service, let's tap into the three spiritual principles of the Gospel of Customer Service. These concepts properly implemented will make any organization a customer service powerhouse.

Principle number one is a **meaningful service vision**. Some of you are wondering, why vision first? It's simple when you understand it. Nothing significant happens until it is first a vision. Vision is the inner picture of what you want to build or be.

You must create a vision of delivering extraordinary customer service to your customers. All great customer service starts with a clear vision or understanding of what great service looks like. Vision is a mental picture of a future state. It is a picture of how you see the organization performing. It is a picture of what you want to be when you grow up. Vision is seeing the end result or the OUT-COME! Why start with a vision? Three powerful reasons:

1. Vision creates focus!

2. Vision identifies direction!

3. Vision unleashes power!

Vision causes you to see the outcome you want in serving your customers. How do you want them to feel? What do you want them to think about your organization? What do you want them to say to others? You must imagine what perfection centered on the customer looks like.

A great visionary illustration of the Gospel of Customer Service is the old classic story of the goose that laid the golden eggs. While taking care of the goose, which is analogous with production capability, the farmer's focus or vision was pure so he reaped a harvest of golden eggs. Greed then took over and filled his visionary capacity. Greed became his focus. What happened when greed took over? The farmer killed the goose to get the eggs out all at once. The result: a dead goose and no more golden eggs. The customer or guest is like the goose that lays the golden eggs! Greed will always cause us to focus on the production (eggs of gold) rather than serving the goose, the source of the golden eggs. If you don't take care of the goose (your customers or guests) one day you will find a shortage of golden eggs (money). Many customer service people "kill the goose" daily by not taking great care of the customer and cannot seem to understand what happened to their golden eggs. In religious work we often call a time of fasting and prayer for financial breakthrough when the root of our problem is mediocre customer service!

Remember, the customer is the reason for the organization. Take a look at the power-point screen:

Four Levels of Customer Service

1. **Customer satisfaction**—minimum requirement for survival.

2. **Customer expectations exceeded**—minimum requirement for growth.

3. **Customer delighted!**—The chief aim of world-class organizations.

4. **CUSTOMER IN WONDER AND AMAZEMENT!**—Goal of The Gospel of Customer Service and the key to rapid growth and profitability.

A VISION OF EXCELLENCE

Vision may sound hyper spiritual, but it is hard-nosed business sense to start with a vision. Look at this point. Every great customer service organization started with vision:

- J. Willard Marriott—Marriott Hotels

- John W. Nordstrom—Nordstrom

- Sam Walton—Wal-Mart

- William Hewlett & David Packard—Hewlett Packard

- Thomas Watson, Sr.—IBM

- Walt Disney—Disneyland, Disney-World Theme Parks

Oscar reminded his class, "At EXCELLENT WAY AUTOMOTIVE GROUP, we have a vision of service excellence—we call it the Gospel of Customer Service! Remember that the word gospel means good news, and it's certainly good news to have our customers become raving fans so that we hear Kaching! Kaching! Kaching! We don't abuse our customers and make lame excuses like THE DEVIL MADE ME DO IT!!!!"

Write the vision and make it plain so that *he may run that reads it.* Oscar pointed to a success poster on the wall and said, "Even Aristotle taught excellence. He said,

EXCELLENCE

"Excellence is an act won by training and habituation. We do not act rightly because we have virtue or excellence, but rather we have those because we have acted rightly. We are what we repeatedly do. Excellence, then, is not an act, but a habit."
—Aristotle

We believe that *love is excellence in action.* We endeavor to serve our guests with love. That's where we derive the name EXCELLENT WAY." Joe thought this was pretty clever. "Sir", said Joe, "Have you ever read Tom Peters book, In

Search Of Excellence? I thought you adapted the name from that classic." Oscar said, "Tom has a fine book and I have read it. That's been many years ago. But the word excellence has always intrigued me wherever I heard it. I saved my resources to buy my first three used automobiles. I then incorporated in the name EXCELLENT WAY and the rest is history." "Wow! You have over one hundred acres of inventory and facilities here. You mean all of this started with just three vehicles?" "No, it actually started with a *VISION*, and a lot of help from the Lord, called the power to get wealth." Joe thought to himself, what a concept.

VISION DEMANDS IMAGINATION

Oscar asked the class to listen closely as he said, "IMAGINATION—the greatest nation in the world! A great service vision is often a result of using your creative imagination to develop a customer friendly vision. Take a moment and imagine a world evangelized with the gospel of customer service excellence, saturated with excellent customer service. Get a vision!"

...And now nothing shall be restrained from them, which they have imagined to do.

Genesis 11: 6

"Imagine"
Some people look at things that are and ask why?
Imagine things that aren't and ask why not?
George Bernard Shaw

COMMITMENT TO SERVICE

Oscar explained to the trainees that we have learned a company with a vision of customer service excellence believes that it exists to serve the customer. Vision means a Commitment to Service! Dedicate yourself to learning the essential practices of a commitment to service and make a commitment to incorporate these practices into the work of organization. "The key is the staff's freedom to focus on the vision: customer service excellence under all circumstances!" Oscar said, "Let's get a lesson from Wal-Mart. Sam Walton, the founder and builder of the Wal-Mart Empire, had his vision right! He said, "*The real boss is always the customer. And he can fire us at anytime by simply deciding to spend his money somewhere else.*"

"Understand that you are the source of your customer service vision because your vision is birthed out of your values! What are your real values?" Oscar then shared with the group a stack of little blue cards. "Here is a values based vision builder. I call it the Gospel of Customer Service motto." The card read:

Always do more than is expected of you.
Always go the extra mile.
If you do, customers will remember you, tell others about you, and come back again and again!

VALUES BASED VISION

One of my favorite quotes is: **"The difference between ordinary and extraordinary is that little extra!"** Extraordinary customer service goes way beyond the norm. A meaningful service vision will make you extraordinary. Because the service is extraordinary, customers talk about it. As customers talk about the service, it sets a standard for the associates of the company, including its leadership, to live up to. It also establishes a benchmark for the industry and, eventually, for business in general! AT EXCELLENT WAY AUTOMOTIVE GROUP, we have learned by precept and practice that service only becomes significant when it is so meaningful to your customers that they articulate and proclaim it! We have found that great values are critical to a great vision.

Oscar explained it this way. A great vision contains three basic ingredients: first, a vision or vision statement; secondly, a mission or mission statement; third, values listed in rank order. Values must be ranked or employees won't know what is more or less important when trying to make a decision that relates to the customer. At EXCELLENT WAY, our values are clearly defined and in rank order. They are 1) Excellence, 2) Effectiveness and 3) Extraordinary Results. All of our people know that excellence, which is love manifested in quality and distinction, is first. LOVE COMES FIRST because love never fails.

VALUES are the foundation for vision. Here are ten possible values as an example of a values list. To be effective, an organization must choose three to five top values.

The following words are examples of core values and organization can choose. They are Love, Integrity, Success, Excellence, Winning, Hard Work, Intelligence, Morality, Service and Effectiveness. Oscar looked the group over and said, "Let's take a brief break before lunch—I don't want you to drift and miss this critical lesson."

Oscar welcomed the class back with a little *name that tune* trivia, by playing a small section of popular 70's tune and gave a box of See's Chocolates to the winner. "Now that I have your attention let's get back to the knitting."

General market research reveals that it costs six times as much to get new customers as it does to keep old ones. If you are serious about customers, you should think deeply on that statement and fact! You could say the success of your organization is determined by your quality ranking in the marketplace. "Quality" is defined by the product or service...plus the way it is delivered. Wisdom dictates that we make our organizations and services of the highest possible quality!

"Great session! Let's take a one hour lunch break."

TOM TREADWELL

After returning to class Oscar said, "I learned years ago that teaching is telling, but training is showing. This afternoon I want to *show* you a real life example of how the power of vision can transform a person from being a car dog to being a customer service pro. We are going to visit one of our best service writers, Tom Treadwell, in the EXCELLENT WAY service department. Tom Treadwell will show you where the rubber meets the road in our vision." Joe said, "That sounds like fun." Oscar told the trainees to leave their books in the training room, but to bring a pen and notebook as they headed joyfully down the stairwell to the service department.

As they all entered the busy, beautiful, air-conditioned service department, one trainee said, "This is no ordinary shop and this floor is so clean you can eat off of it." A bubbly tall, handsome, dark haired gentleman came dashing from behind a counter and said, "It's A GREAT DAY AT EXCELLENT WAY! I'm Tom Treadwell. How can I be of service to you all?" Oscar stepped out of the group and said, "Hi Tom. I have some new recruits that we are showing the WAY." "Oh Mr. Paywell, I didn't see you. This is the class I met at orientation. At first I thought I had a tour group from one of our local colleges coming through again." Oscar said, "Thanks Tom, but just call me Oscar. I want you to take a little time as usual and tell these people about the transforming power of vision. I'll be back in about forty-five minutes. I have an interview waiting. Gotta keep the pipeline filled with good people you know." "At your service Mr., oops, I mean, Oscar. They are in good hands with Treadwell."

Tom turned to the class. "One of the first things I had to learn when I came here to work is the power of a vision to transform your heart. I have now been here for ten years. I had worked for five other dealerships over a span of four years and learned all of the bad habits you can imagine. I was truly what we call in our industry a car dog. Mad at the world and ready to bite, scream or cuss when I felt a customer was trying to get the upper hand on me." Joe asked, "How did you change?" Tom answered, "The Great Awakening! The Apostle and the Gospel of Customer Service caused me to awake to treating customers right. This awareness of my old way helped me change to the MORE EXCELLENT WAY. You could say I saw the light and repented!"

"Oscar did a class back in those days called Transformation Training. First, he taught about the heart—A change of heart is often the birth of a vision. This is a change from the inside out. The change is a desire to serve people. You See it, Size it, and then Seize it! Then, he said the change affects your head. You think about it constantly. Finally, it affects the hands. You start to use you heart, head, and hand to serve your guests with excellence.

Tom then told the class there is a customer service crisis from coast to coast. The word "crisis" to the Chinese means "danger, yet opportunity." We have a great opportunity today, since service everywhere is so bad, by offering extraordinary service.

Service in most car dealerships and businesses is so bad today that people expect to be abused. Have you had any poor service lately?" Several in the group nodded yes and others said out loud, "Sure have!" "Here are some areas of mediocre service that are almost the norm: *dirty restrooms, late deliveries, lost product orders, unkind cashiers, rude greeters, lazy staff, broken promises...* At EXCELLENT WAY we focus on operating in The Gospel of Customer Service and this gives us a definite edge in the 21st century."

We don't want satisfied customers but AMAZED customers!

THE RIGHT VISION

"At EXCELLENT WAY AUTOMOTIVE GROUP, we are big fans of Dr. Ken Blanchard. In fact, it was his book Raving Fans and his FAITHWALK Leadership program that really got Oscar turned on to the theory of serving customers. We call Raving Fans our customer service Bible. It's required reading for all of our employees. Ken has a part in every excellence award we have ever won.

Dr. Blanchard has another excellent book written with Jesse Stoner; "Full Steam Ahead." This book makes *the vision thing* plain. In it, Ken says the three key elements of a compelling vision are: First, significant purpose, then clear values and finally a picture of the future.

The Power of the Right Vision does several things. It attracts commitment and energizes people, creates meaning in workers lives, establishes a standard of excellence and bridges the present and the future."

Tom moved to a large poster saying, "Here is an example of an empowering Vision":

> *Our Vision:*
> *To Be An Ever Expanding And Vital Market Vehicle For Use By God To Work In The Lives Of People As They Serve And Contribute To Others.*
> **ServiceMaster®**

After Oscar saw the light he decided to do some research to find out how to develop the right vision for our service department. He thought to himself what would happen if I made my dealership the Service Master of the automobile business in our area? WOW! Through personal investigation and surveys he found that:

    30 % of customers thought service hours were inconvenient
    50% thought labor prices were too high
    47% said they had to wait too long while having service done
    58% thought the service writer lacked people skills

Tom then said, "Oscar decided to focus his vision and make Excellent Way a cut above the competition in all of these crucial areas and the rest is history. Our service business is booming! We even have a waiting list for oil changes because of our reputation of convenient hours, great prices, and prompt service."

VISION OF PERFECTION

I always strive for perfection when dealing with my service guests on the service drive. To be the best you must strive for perfection. Some say lighten up to perfection, nobody's perfect. Here is something I learned at a training class that will help.

Why Perfection?

Let's say perfection is 100% so even 99.9% would not be good enough.

Why? If 99.9% were good enough:

- *22,000 checks will be deducted from the wrong bank account in the next 60 minutes.*
- *1,314 phone calls will be displaced by telecommunication services every minute.*
- *12 babies will be given to the wrong parents each day.*
- *268,500 defective tires will be shipped this year.*
- *20,000 incorrect drug prescriptions will be written in the next 12 months.*

Customer contact people must use their own imagination in conjunction with management to create a vision of perfection that fits within the organization's structure based on the customer's needs. This builds self-esteem and its fun! Resolve to give the best customer service of any person or organization in the world. Decide what excellent customer service would be and get started."

Tom told the class, "It's been about forty-five minutes and you can bet your bottom dollar Oscar will be coming down any minute now." Joe Simple said, "I am amazed at how in-sync you are with Oscar and his teachings, and how in tune this whole place is with this interesting Church I attended with a friend months ago." Tom said, "That's the transforming power of catching, carrying, and communicating a vision. When people have the same vision, they are in sync, as you put it Joe."

"Now", Tom said, "Oscar has taught us five practical steps I want to share with you. This is a critical piece of information I call vision action steps."

1.   Develop and communicate a clear vision.

2. Make certain that no jobs are labeled "Customer Service." Service is everyone's job.

3. Be alert to what makes customers happy, and then apply it.

4. Train all staff members in customer service basics.

5. Keep the vision of service excellence before you and your people!

Oscar decided that he would do some serious studying to find out what customers wanted in a service writer here is what he found. We call it the Excellent Way Magic Five.

1. A person that shows courtesy.

2. A person that smiles.

3. A person that's honest.

4. A person that's knowledgeable.

5. A person that follows through and follows up.

While he was still chatting, Oscar came bouncing in and said, "Thanks Tom for your investment in our new class. Your labor is not in vain." "You're welcome boss."

Oscar took the class back up to the training room and dismissed them for the day. "Another wonderful day", Joe thought as he headed to his BMW to hit the local Starbucks.

As Joe walked into Starbucks he looked on the wall above the counter in the workers line of sight and saw a poster that said,

"For some reason, your customers seem to get better when you get better!"

Joe thought this was very interesting. "I'm seeing this customer service excellence stuff everywhere I go now! **I believe I am catching the VISION!"**

Summary of Spiritual Principle #1 "A Meaningful Service Vision"

- Service starts with a vision
- Create a clear vision of perfection centered on the customer
- Vision must align with values
- A clear vision puts us in sync with others
- You must catch, carry, and communicate the vision

10

TRAINING DAY—TWO

✦

Customer Oriented People

SPIRITUAL PRINCIPLE #2:
"Customer Oriented PEOPLE"

Oscar welcomed the group with an energetic, "Good Morning! Now it's time to get into the heart of the Gospel of Customer Service by looking closely at the second principle. We call it **Customer Oriented People.** Walt Disney said, *"You can dream, create, design and build the most wonderful place in the world…but it requires people to make the dream a reality."AMEN WALT!*

Customer oriented people have a radical, fanatical, and relentless focus on the customer! At EXCELLENT WAY we only hire customer-oriented people. We don't hire people we have to tell to be nice to the customer; we hire nice people! Why? You must understand AND SERVE the desires of the customer to win in today's competitive marketplace. The Gospel of Customer Service will give the customer service rep insight and understanding of what customers generally want.

Here are some vital questions to ask yourself:

- Who are your key customers today?
- In the future?
- What are their expectations for service quality?

You must discover the *customer's vision* and then alter your vision, if need be." Oscar said, "We teach and train our people to always remember that *doing things well that are not important to the customer has no impact!"*

Oscar then asked the class, "How do you find out what customers want?" One trainee said, "Study market trends." Another said, "Examine buying habits." Joe said, "This may sound super simple but, ask them!" "Mr. Simple you are simply brilliant! It's so simple most MBA students miss that one. Always remember, you have not because you ask not…

Let me illustrate. I was watching our own Atlanta Falcons play the Cleveland Browns in a pre-season game and the commentator was asking the V.P. of Marketing, How did you guys make history by selling out the Falcons season. His response blew me away. He said, "Arthur Blank simply asked the fans what they wanted and tried to accommodate them. The result? A sold out Georgia Dome and the Falcons are leading the league in team sportswear sales." Oscar said, "That sure isn't rocket science, is it? Here are some sample questions. Ask, "How can we better serve you?" You can also ask, "How can we improve our services in the future?" When they answer, always say, "We'll get on that right away!"

Oscar sat down on the training table and said, "Let's have a heart to heart about relating to customers in a friendship relationship. I call this "customers and you." Customer retention is the key to organizational success. Customer retention is what we call a "critical success factor". Single visit guests are too hard and expensive to acquire. Your focus must be on the second and third visit. The organization's goal: resale to the same customer over and over. Customer retention is a major key to continued growth of a business or ministry. In the automobile business, most of my colleagues have a saying that there are no such things as be-backs! A be-back is a customer that did not buy, but promised you he would BE-BACK. Many even humorously, yet seriously say the be-back bus has broken down. At EXCELLENT WAY, we have a 65% be-back closing ratio. (Be-backs that bought automobiles) We believe in be-back and repeat buyers.

Here are some samples of what customers want:

- **FRIENDLY CHEERFUL SERVICE**

- **PROMPTNESS OF SERVICE, DELIVERY AND BILLING**

- **EASE OF TRANSACTIONS**

- **CONVENIENCE AND NO HASSLE**

They also want quick responses to problems and complaints, and to be valued, appreciated and made to feel important. *This can only be accomplished with customer-oriented people.* Service legends have learned to set minimum standards for customer service and hire customer friendly people.

THE POWER OF WOM!

Oscar continued, "Customer oriented people relating to the customer in a positive manner releases THE POWER OF W.O.M. (Word Of Mouth)."

Negative talk that is true is especially damaging to an organization. Word of Mouth is the major influence in the market today. Word of mouth, what people are saying about your business, is the most powerful and inexpensive source of advertising. Your aim is to deliver with such excellence that customers start bragging about you, releasing the power of WOM.

Your method: Customer Service Excellence by speedy response to inquiries, fast action on complaints, regular follow-up and continuous service. WOW!

Our major measure of success at EXCELLENT WAY is the percentage of business from repeat sales and referrals. Imagine if a company could not market and advertise anymore. What would happen to the business? The key to getting repeat and referral business is to **treat every customer as if you were on the verge of losing him or her!**

Customers that are treated like kings and queens by customer-oriented people become fans of the business. I'm amazed by the amount of businesses that can't see this. I think they are blinded by the *cash bottom line*. I like what Ken Blanchard teaches about the bottom line. It's smart stuff. Ken says with passion, there's a triple bottom line: Gung Ho people that act like they own the place, Raving Fan Customers that brag about the organization and Big Bucks—financial profitability. Here are some reasons for customer defection: lack of attention, indifference on the part of someone in the company, lack of responsiveness to inquiries, and lack of responsiveness to complaints. Remember, Fast Response Builds Loyalty! Oscar then said, "Check out this concept."

Golden Rule: serve your customers the way you would like to be served!

Golden Chain: develop an endless chain of referrals and repeat customers.

USAA (United States Automobile Association) is a great example of excellent customer service through customer friendly people. They have come out with ten PRIDE principles that all of their employees know and live by:

1. *Exceed customer expectations.*

2. *Live the Golden Rule.*

3. *Be a leader.*

4. *Participate and contribute.*

5. *Pursue Excellence.*

6. *Work as a team.*

7. *Share knowledge.*

8. *Keep it simple.*

9. *Listen and communicate.*

10. *Have fun!*

Oscar then said to his trainees, "The big question you must answer is; what do your customers think about your service and people? If you are in business that is the most important question you can answer! As you can plainly see, the customer could be your best critic, if only you would let them speak up! The fact is most customers don't take the time to let someone know when they are unhappy. They harbor resentment and at some point simply choose to take their business somewhere else.

A statistic I want you to always remember is; "FOR EVERY CUSTOMER THAT COMPLAINS, TWENTY SIX DON'T!" It is imperative that you understand what your customers think and what they expect from you! Remember it is their choice to do business with you! Research reveals that you must make the customers feel at ease about complaining if you want honest feedback." After this intense session Oscar said, "Some of you are starting to get that glazed-over look." "Oh no, we are just soaking in the seriousness of customer service", Joe said. "As you talked, I was thinking, the way I treat customers affects everything in my life, including my five year old daughter's college education. This is great content. I would have never expected this quality of training in a car dealership." Oscar then said, "Thanks for your kind comments Joe. Alright! Take a break, get a bottle of water, piece of the fruit or beef jerky from the training snack table and I'll see you in fifteen minutes."

After the workshop, nobody moved from their seat. So, Oscar looked the group over and started singing the old Mc Donald's jingle. *You deserve a break today...*I'll see you...

Upon returning from the break Oscar said, "I have a gift for the person that can tell me the three spiritual principles of the gospel of customer service. Please raise your hands!" Joe quickly raised his hands, stood up and said:

- A Meaningful Service **VISION**

- Customer Oriented **PEOPLE**

- Customer Friendly **SYSTEMS**

Oscar said, "That's excellent Joe! Here's a twenty-five dollar gift certificate to Starbucks Coffee!" Joe said, "Mama Mia! STARBUCKS!!! It pays to pay attention!"

Oscar said, "Remember class—Vision, People, Systems. I like it! I like it! I think you are getting it now! I want you to drive home today saying *Vision, People & Systems!*" One student said, "I find it easy to remember things in three's, just like lions, and tigers, and bears—what does that make you guys think about?" "The Wiz," said a young trainee that had not said a word until now! "The Wizard of Oz is our family favorite and my dad said he has watched it since he was a tot." Oscar said with a smile, "If you can remember that, you can remember the three principles of service excellence." The young student said, "Yeah, but I have seen the Wizard of Oz fifty times." Oscar said, "Hint, hint. Repetition is the seed of learning and the mother of skill!"

Vision! People! Systems!

A CULTURE SHOCK!

Your corporate culture has everything to do with how customer oriented your people are. Even if you bring customer oriented people into a bad culture they are often brought down by the negativity. Here are five steps to transforming your culture into a customer service giant. We eat, drink and breathe these at EXCELLENT WAY!

1. **Create the culture you desire.**

   How clear are your standards on what behaviors and attitudes are acceptable?

   Most employees are willing to do what's asked of them as long as it is reasonable.

   The grumpy boss coming down on others for a poor attitude toward customers is the ultimate oxymoron! The key to your culture is: WALK YOUR TALK!

2. **Empower Your Staff!**

   Knowledge. The more people understand about the company, the philosophies, marketing strategies and goals, the more effective they will be in delivering the level of service you desire. Do the organization's employees understand the vision, mission, and values? Do they know what it costs to acquire a new customer?

3. **Provide skills development training.**

   Most companies do not train their staff on the customer service skills.

   Most people have never been taught or trained in people skills, the basics of human relationships. **Customer service is all about human relationships.**

4. **Coach everyone!**

   Communication is the key to success! It is crucial that employees and managers have a clear understanding of their performance expectations and how they are going to achieve them. Reinforce positive behaviors and modify negative behaviors.

5. **Repeat the sounding Praise!**

An environment of praise is conducive to customer service excellence.

An environment of criticism is counter-productive to great customer service!

The major principle here is what Dr. Ken Blanchard calls Gung Ho! A Gung Ho environment is charged with enthusiasm and energy and the energy will be transferred to the customer. To have Raving Fan customers, you must first have Gung Ho people!

As **customer oriented people,** we continually focus on what customers want. People are the key to customer service, not inventory systems or fancy computers. PEOPLE! Customers come in with needs; people meet those needs by friendly service, use of tools, and use of technology. But don't lose sight of the human factor. At EXCELLENT WAY, our people are truly our greatest asset. Not our elaborate building, our multi-million dollar inventory, or our state of the art computer system. PEOPLE, FOLKS, INDIVIDUALS!!! One by one, many companies let people go by the hundreds every year to protect the owner's yacht fund, or some other material perk of the top dogs! People serve customers, not things. Just ask Sam Walton, Walt Disney, Thomas Watson Sr. (IBM's founder). Read about these service legends if you are serious about outstanding service. I think those giants would turn over in their graves if they saw how poor customer service has gotten. WOE TO THE CUSTOMER SERVICE AGENT or so-called business that just keeps saying THE DEVIL MADE ME DO IT!

Henry Royce once heard a technician working on a difficult problem say, "That's good enough". Some reports say some of the other workers had to physically hold Mr. Royce off of the man. Nothing was good enough! That's a man with a passion for serving people. I want to shout it in the market, in the C.E.O.s conference room, in the sales meeting: People, People, People! As Sly would say EVERYDAY PEOPLE!"

One student said, "Oscar, I think you missed your calling, hint, hint." Oscar just smiled real big. He then put on a humorous, professional voice and said, "Empirical studies and profound knowledge give us the intellectual insight that customers often determine how good you are based on regular, ongoing service."

Here are some factors that research reveals are important to customers:

- *Quality at every turn*
- *Solutions to problems*
- *Solve customer needs*
- *Solve and deal with confrontations*
- *Quick response.* Be quick to respond.
- *Be at your post!*—Customers hate arriving at a counter and not finding any help.
- *Excellent service after the sale.*

> "At most car dealerships the most abused customer is the sold customer. We give excellent service after the sale!"
> —Bernard Smalls

GETTING INTO YOUR CUSTOMER'S SOUL

At EXCELLENT WAY AUTOMOTIVE we have learned that it is crucial to get into your customer's soul and make sure you are doing a good job! Joe said, "The word soul just seems a little strong for customer service. Isn't there a better, softer word we can use?" Oscar responded, "Actually Joe, the word soul does not mean what most people think. Some people think of soul music and get images of Tina Turner rocking the house. Religious people think of the eternal human spirit. The word soul means mind, will and emotions. Does this make more sense now?" Joe said, "Yeah, you got me for a moment. Thanks for the clarity."

How do you get into the customer's soul? You ask them for honest feedback and the customer tells you. Another way is to do surveys or questionnaires.

Ask specific questions, not questions like, *"Are you happy?"* Get specific!

Here are some sample questions to ask.
What are your expectations of us? How are we doing?
How can I increase the value of my service today?
The most important question to improve on: *"If you could think of one thing that could have made it even better, what would it be?"*
Then you must listen…

Be swift to hear, slow to speak…

NO MORE LOYALTY?

Oscar said "Many business leaders and managers are saying there is no more loyalty in the marketplace, especially in the automobile business. But I have found that you can create loyal customers, if you know how to use your resources and turn dissatisfaction into loyalty. There is a key to loyalty and this is it. **Loyalty in today's competitive market must be created!** Pull out your thinking caps and let's be creative."

- How can you recognize your customers in special, personalized ways?
- In what ways have you been able to implement customer service innovation in your job?
- How could your organization's customer service become more ideal?
- Do everything in your power to solve a problem immediately.

Use the "I think this is the best way" method. It's better than, "This is the only way." Do something extra for the customer. After you solve the problem, do something more. If possible, do something extraordinary. Remember: Questions are the greatest customer service tool. The better you become at asking questions, the easier it will be for you to become a Customer Service Pro and create Loyalty.

Oscar walked to his large flipchart and displayed the sheet that read:

"Seek first to understand, then to be understood…"

—Steven Covey, 7 Habits of Highly Effective People

In designing services, we need to remember above all else that our logic is not necessarily the same as the customer's logic. Losing sight of the customer's logic can lead your organization to become introverted. Employees who don't understand the services they deliver in holistic terms, easily get caught up in methods and procedures and lose sight of the effect their organizational apparatus has on the customer. Insisting that your customer follow complicated procedures for the benefit of the organization is dumb!

"THE CUSTOMER'S PERCEPTION IS EVERYTHING!"

SOLUTIONS CREATE LOYALTY

Oscar went on to say that to create loyalty you must understand that customers want solutions above all else. Here are five factors in the execution of solutions.

1. You must choose the best solution, always without fail.

2. Use the word *"recommend."* Tailor the recommendation to the customer's needs, not yours.

3. Give the customer confidence—not so much because of your knowledge about policies or procedures, but because you are able to access what you know and apply it in terms and services that are meaningful to the customer.

4. Involve your customer in the solution.

5. Don't use technical or spiritual terms. The customer wants simple straightforward solutions not Greek, Hebrew or Hi-tech terms.

At EXCELLENT WAY, we always treat customer complaints with the utmost urgency. Most customers believe that we as dealers are all about sales and no service. So our attention to details concerning customer complaints makes us stand out from the pack. Oscar said, "I love this job!"

We teach and train our people that no matter what happens, continue to make your customers feel important. Never let the customer think that you have anything more important to do than be with him or her at that moment—especially as you move toward the conclusion of your conversation. Pay special attention to small details. Little, apparently insignificant, differences between your organization and your competitors can mean everything. Recognize and capitalize your slight edge through fanatical attention to details. Remember in a negative world "The Devil is in the details…" In the Gospel of Customer Service we say GOD IS IN THE DETAILS☺!

CUSTOMERS WANT STRONGER RELATIONSHIPS

Oscar said, "Now that we have a pretty good handle on the principle of complaint resolutions, we need to know and remember that RELATIONSHIPS COUNT! Research reveals that most customers want stronger relationships with the people they do business with. This creates the trust factor. Since there are so many products and services in the highly competitive marketplace, most customers are looking for someone they can trust. The friendship factor is one of the most powerful factors in business, especially in selling."

> *"Seventy one percent of people buy from you because they like you, respect you, and trust you!"*
> —New York Management Club Study

Oscar shared a story with the group about a friend who was a former pro football player that had gone through his relationship based training at his dealership, but moved away and went to work for a local dealership. The friend said to the interviewer, "I have been trained in relationship based selling and…," before he could finish the statement, the interviewing manger said, "Now listen! I don't go for that soft stuff. Our philosophy here is simple. Put the screws to them before they put the screws you." My friend took the job out of desperation but soon quit the dealership and went into another type of business. Here are some simple ways to build stronger relationships. Manage the first impressions! You never get a second chance to make a first impression! Knowledge of your business! General knowledge—a little about a lot of things! Enthusiasm! Imagination!

Oscar's timer started to beep and he said, "Let's take a well-deserved break! See you in fifteen minutes."

GEORGE GOODWRENCH

All Customer Oriented people have Attitudes of Excellence! To best communicate this, I want to take you all on a field trip to our parts department to meet George Goodwrench. George, like Tom Treadwell, is one of our customer service stars at EXCELLENT WAY. George Goodwrench will give you the nuts and bolts of tightening up your mental attitude. He is Mr. Positive Service Attitude. Let's go…

As they walked into the parts department, they all noticed a motivational poster that said: *Attitudes of Excellence = Customer Service Excellence.* A well-built, handsome, African American man came out from his office when he saw a group gathering at the parts counter. With a bright smile he said, "It's a great day at EXCELLENT WAY! How can I serve you?" Oscar was purposefully hiding behind a pillar, so when he heard George's greeting, he popped out and said, "Surprise George! I have a wonderful group of trainees for you to chat with. Remember you met them at this week's orientation along with Tom and Sally." "Of course, how could I forget such a good-looking group?" said George. "They really cheered us on in the training room as shining stars." Oscar said, "I need to go to the fitness center and check out the big screen Sony. Some of the workers say it went out during Sports Center late last night. We will have it repaired or replaced before the technicians and the clean up crew get off so they can enjoy their workout more. I'll see you in about an hour." George took the trainees into a big open area, pulled up a flip chart and started to share…

George said to the group, "Most people don't realize that the parts department is a business within a business. We must meet and greet customers with a smile, listen to their needs, sell them product and deliver outstanding customer service. Here are seven things that I teach all of my parts people about customer service.

1. Friendly meeting and greeting

2. Always introduce yourself

3. Firm enthusiastic handshakes

4. Acknowledge customers even when you are busy

5. Listen attentively with good body language

6. Don't rush the customer

7. Professionalism (look and act like a pro)

I know you folks will be in sales but I at least wanted to introduce you to a part of our philosophy so that you understand why we do what we do. In the average dealership, the turf wars prevail and parts and sales are archenemies. At EXCELLENT WAY we work together. Now let's take a look at *Attitudes.*"

ATTITUDES & ALTITUDES!

George said, "I really like to call this part of the training "Attitudes & Altitudes." At EXCELLENT WAY AUTOMOTIVE GROUP, we believe that your attitude in customer service controls our altitude in the market place. I have found that most managers reprimand people and just say; *get your attitude right*, without ever really teaching and training frontline people on what a good attitude looks like. Remember that all excellent customer service starts with understanding what a good job looks like. Get this point guys—Your Attitude Controls Your Altitude!

Frontline employees must develop an attitude of integrity. Integrity is: Authenticity, fairness, ethics and consistency. Many in our business believe that it is all about the money. We believe that money is a result of wealth of character, ethics and principles. We embrace what Ken Blanchard said in his wonderful book, Big Bucks—**Profit Is That Applause You Get for Taking Care of the Customer.**"

Joe said, "George that sounds good, but how do you operate in integrity and not go broke in today's competitive markets. Every body lies in business today, particularly when buying or selling a car. In the I.T. business my old boss use to operate in situational integrity. Meaning he told the truth as long as it didn't cost him a deal or a contract. He use to say *that's the way it is because—BUSINESS IS BUSINESS!*" George said to Joe, "I appreciate your honesty. Many in the automotive business believe that if you can't let lies roll off of your tongue with a straight face, you just aren't a good car man. They feel that a good liar is synonymous with a good car man. But we are the number one volume dealer in Atlanta and all of our deals are integrity based. We believe in the old saying "the truth will always out live a lie." To give real service, you must add something which cannot be bought or measured with money, and that is sincerity and integrity."

INTEGRITY BASED SERVICE

Here are some principles on how to express integrity in service:

1. Commitment to the win-win dynamic. If something is good for the customer, it has to be good for the organization.

2. High productivity. When you love what you do, you find the energy to do it well.

3. High quality. If your heart is in something, you will do the best with the highest possible standards.

4. High standards. If you pursue integrity in all that you do, you will not slack off.

5. Lots of fun. Can you have passion without enthusiasm? Enthusiasm means to be imbued with spirit—God within. If God is within your conscience, you will have an inward pull toward integrity. When you operate by integrity, it won't be dull.

6. Consistency without conformity. Adherence to a strong set of standards, which promote ownership and creativity.

7. Have your heart in your work and your work in your heart!

We are in business for one reason, to serve society!

FRONTLINE ATTITUDES

George then moved back to another chart that said, "The Attitude of Personal Excellence must be developed because you do not inherently put the customer first!"

Frontline Employees are the key to great customer service because problems are best solved at the point of the problem. Outstanding Customer Service demands that you go the extra mile with… The Right Mental Attitude. Attitudes control Altitudes! Edison said, "Greatness is an ordinary man with an extraordinary Attitude!" Now, let's focus on this attitude/altitudes concept in some specific areas. Let's look at some areas we need to work on.

The first is **"Attitude in the Workplace"**. The glad attitude is contagious in the workplace. I firmly believe that what Wally "Famous" Amos said is true. He said, "Whatever you see on the screen of life was first seen in your mind. If you don't like what you see, change the reel of film, change your attitude, and change your thoughts". We need to renew the spirits of our minds, developing a fresh mental and spiritual attitude. To truly be happy you must do what you love—love what you do!" Ken Blanchard says—"If you want to make Big Bucks, Love Thy Work or Try Las Vegas!"

Happiness in the workplace is the major key to providing superior customer service. None of this training works to its maximum potential without happiness in the workplace. Service is demanding. Service inherently breaks down, if those delivering it are not happy. People need to be given space to provide truly outstanding customer service. Managers must give people room to grow and to encourage it. Support and encouragement are a mental safety net for happiness. *Give people room to be outstanding!*

The second attitude we want to look at is the **"Attitude of Teamwork."**

George then said to the group, "We must come to value the wisdom of developing high performing teams. Start to use the terminology Our Company. I'm sure that some of you have studied psychology at one time or another. In just about any good book on empirical psychology you will find Maslow's Hierarchy of Human Needs. Abraham Maslow taught that humans have five basic needs that fall into an order or hierarchy. They are Physiology, Safety, Social, Self-Esteem, and Self-Actualization. Self-actualization is becoming all you should be and the highest need of humans. It also relates to belonging to something great and serving others. We are really here to serve others, and that is where we find our greatest fulfillment or, as Maslow puts it, Self-Actualization. Belonging to something grand is the greatest of human needs—develop team thinking in the *workplace!* Here are some team building principles:"

Give others what they want first. People will generally work hard for emotional benefits and recognition, in addition to the monetary income.

Show respect for others. The courtesy you express to other team members generally sets the example for the respect you show to your customers.

Make other team members feel important. Human Resource professionals insist that as much as 90% of things we do in life are fueled by a desire to feel important. Seek ways to be a genuine cheerleader.

Offer positive feedback. William James, one of the world's best-known psychologists once said, "The desire to be appreciated is one of the deepest drives in human nature.

Do simple favors for others." The Harvard Business School conducted an extensive test to determine how successful people earn the respect and cooperation of their coworkers. They found that one of the most effective techniques—developing a knack for doing simple favors—was the easiest and least costly.

Use names. This has been mentioned previously in terms of your conversations with external customers. This should certainly be in your relationships with team members!

The third and final attitude to develop is The **"Attitude of a Peace Maker"**. Joe said, "Now come on George. That sounds a little too spiritual for the workplace. In a results-driven numbers game like the car business, who has time to be a peacemaker? I was taught to get it done and be a pacemaker." "Well Joe, the Book says, "blessed are the peacemakers", not the pacemakers. I must say that in our industry most car dogs only care about numbers and the cash. In many dealerships, you can have the owner's firstborn if you sell enough cars for him. We believe that our business is empowered to prosper when our people avoid getting into internal politics and strife, which comes from trying to climb the ladder of sales at the expense of positive relationships in the workplace. We are a business, but we are also a team and a family, if you will. The Book also says in James 3: 16, "For where envy and strife is, there is confusion and every evil work." When you get into politics and strife you will not be thinking about the customer, but about yourself. Three types of employees that will not serve customers well:

1. Politicians—striving for recognition and promotion

2. Egotist—blinded by self interests

3. Freeloaders—looking for a free lunch.

The fatal flaw in customer service—Selfishness!!! Being so focused on what you want to happen that you lose sight of what the customer wants to happen. Selfish people carry a negative mental attitude! Zig Ziglar says, "It's your **attitude,** not your **aptitude** that controls your **altitude!"**

Joe said to George, "I understand where you are coming from with all this attitude stuff, but my understanding of the car business is that it's a cash cow. You milk it for money. We sell cars for money, don't we? The bottom line is money. I was taught back in New Jersey that there are three reasons to go to work; MONEY, MONEY, MONEY!" George said, "You know Joe, I am a musician and we did an opening once for The O'Jays. The first song they did that night was the 70's oldie but goodie, Money, Money, Money…great beat, great music. A timeless proverbs says; "loving favor is more valuable than silver or gold." In fact if you are the best, you will gain the favor of your customers and have all the gold you want. Remember that the goose lays the golden egg! Zig Ziglar certainly understands this he said" *You can get anything in life that you want, if you just help enough people get what they want!"*

George said, "Let me ask you folks a question. Does anyone here know what makes most customer service representatives outstanding?" John said, "Raving Fan Service?" "Good try John." Jill said, "An extraordinary attitude?" "Excellent thought Jill." Joe said, "From my training, I believe its communication skills." "BINGO! You got it Joe. Now, let's study how to be outstanding in customer service." George then said, "Just having a positive attitude is not enough to serve customers well. This will help put attitudes into action." George began to give the trainees a list of **The Three V's for Better Communications**:

The First V is Visual First. Remember, "You get no second chance to make a first impression. Clothes don't make the man, but they sure do introduce him. Before you have had a chance to say a word, many people will judge you strictly by your appearance. Your choice of clothing should be suitable for the situation. Always look professional. **Never look sloppy!"**

The Second V is Vocal. Remember, the way you sound in person or on the phone has an impact. Have you ever listened to a monotone? We all have a vocal range to work with. Range rises when we are stressed or under pressure. Most customers prefer listening to calm, lower pitched voices. We can all learn to speak this way.

The Third V is Verbal. To wrap it up on communication, let's talk some about **Verbal** skills. Look in the training manual with me at Verbal Communication Rules: Use descriptive language. Use short sentences. Avoid slang, technical words and jargon. Avoid tag questions and qualifiers. (I guess, probably, sorta…).

We have found at EXCELLENT WAY, that having short and informal conversations with customers can be an effective way to add a friendly touch to your interactions with them. It shows that you are a warm human being and not a robotic customer service representative. Some topics to avoid are controversial subjects like:

> Politics
> Religion
> Ethnic jokes
> Salaries
> Rumors
> Gossip
> Confidential business information
> Negative information about competitors

Oscar had finished with the big screen task in the fitness center and came in to find the class standing around George as he discussed the importance of communication skills. George said, "Let's do a quick check up from the neck up by analyzing how to change your customer service attitude. To improve on your attitude you must become a believer. If necessary you must repent and believe the gospel of customer service. You'll see it when you believe it." George said, "Now, let's go all the way with PMA (Positive Mental Attitude)! The boss is back so I will bow out—here's Oscar!" The group gave him a standing O.

Oscar asked the trainees, "Did George do a good job with his attitude workshop?" They responded one by one and together, "yeah, wonderful, awesome, great!" "Well, let's go back up to the training room and wrap it up." Oscar turned to George and said, "You are certainly making a difference here at EXCELLENT WAY George—Well done! Keep up the good work." "Thanks boss—all the way with PMA!"

As they entered the training room, the trainees found one of the waitresses from the deli standing by a portable ice cream maker. "Ice Cream to end the day for anyone? We have many different flavors and different types of cones." Joe said, "I'll take cappuccino on a chocolate waffle cone." Others started to pipe in their orders. One young lady in the group turned to Oscar and said, "Thanks Mr. Paywell. You have a way of making us feel so special." Oscar smiled and said softly, "You *are* special!"

Oscar said, "I have one thought before leaving (as they were enjoying the gourmet ice cream). Dale Carnegie said when dealing with people, remember you are not dealing with creatures of logic, but with creatures of emotion—creatures bristling with prejudice, and motivated by pride and vanity.

Remember the way you have been served during this training class and do so unto others. Operating in the Gospel of Customer Service means having customers fall in love with our people and organization, so that they begin to brag about us to their family, friends, and associates! *Let's go home; it's been a great day!*"

Summary of Spiritual Principle #2
Customer Oriented People

- Hire nice people.

- Learn to listen to customers.

- If customers are not happy, they are just looking for a way out and they won't come back unless there's nothing better.

- Make sure your priorities are the same as the customers!
- Take care of your customers!

11

TRAINING DAY—THREE

❖

Customer Friendly Systems

SPIRITUAL PRINCIPLE #3:
Customer Friendly **SYSTEMS**

The next morning Oscar came happily into the class. He welcomed the group and said, "I'm excited to see you all again! Let's all stand up and say something positive to start the day! Repeat after me—I FEEL HEALTHY, I FEEL HAPPY, and I FEEL TERRIFIC!" All the trainees stood and repeated the chant widened with amazement. Joe had already heard this before on one of his W. Clement Stone tapes, so he just smiled and thought, "Wow this is great! What a release of energy!"

Oscar said, "It's day three and today we will cover the final principle in the Gospel of Customer Service, which is **Customer Friendly Systems**. Of the three major principles, you will see how customer friendly systems allow you to deliver excellent service. *Consistent Systems Cause Consistent Delivery Which Creates Customers for Life.* The commitment is to design every part of your organization, with service as the desired outcome, so that you exceed the customers' expectations. Jesus taught the Biblical principle about going the extra mile. Customer service is a great opportunity for acting on this concept. In The Gospel of Customer Service you must always go the extra-mile!"

You have heard the old saying, "The road to hell is paved with good intentions". The road to poor performance is paved with the organization's intentions to serve the customer without customer friendly SYSTEMS! Good intentions are not enough! You must have systems! AMEN??? The group said—AMEN!!!

Consistent Delivery is a key customer retention strategy. Consistent delivery demands systems! The organization's major goal should be to deliver such excellent customer service that a solid relationship is developed with guests that return again and again. Customer Friendly Systems will produce outstanding customer service, which cause customers to return again and again!

The only thing that makes our organization stand out from the crowd is The Gospel of Customer Service! Doesn't it make sense in an unstable economy to work harder to retain your customer base, which you have invested thousands of dollars to develop?

The most valuable asset any company has is its customer base! Yet many treat customer service like it's just a slogan. Slogans are ok, but we must go beyond slogans to systems that benefit the customer. Here is an example of a good sounding slogan. Let's examine it.

"The Year of the Customer!"

Oscar said, "Now, let's do a little critical thinking. If this is the year of the customer, what will next year be? You must have systems and not just slogans because, in delivering Customer Service, many things can go wrong, even though you have good intentions, because of the human element."

All legendary service organizations have Customer Friendly Systems. They do the small things to provide a level of service that exceeds customers' expectations. Customer service people need the skills that empower them to take care of customers. Remember, they are the customer contact people. They contact the customer you spend money on advertising to get them into your business. Many organizations, businesses and ministries need to rethink the training budget. Why spend thousands in advertising to have untrained people serve your guests?

Oscar said to his trainees, "We at EXCELLENT WAY know that customer service is a very demanding job. Customers will put you under the microscope when they find that you preach the gospel of Excellent Customer Service. Why is customer service so demanding today? Customer service today is more challenging than ever before. Customers are more educated than ever before. Customers are more knowledgeable about products and services than ever before. Customers are more demanding with regard to quality, service and value. Customers have so many choices and less urgency to make decisions. Customers are impatient and want everything now."

Some customer friendly tactics to meet the demand are to listen to what customers say about your organization. Involve the whole organization in the service process. Respect that customers vote most clearly with their patronage! Hang out where your customers do. Observe your customers being served by others. Relate your customers' experiences to your own. Organize opportunities to pay attention (focus groups, employee site visits, the frontline trained to listen and communicate feedback). Create the customer service point of view for all staff members. **Seek to exceed expectations!**

SALLY SELLERS

Oscar said, "Now to bring service into perspective, I want to present to you our real expert in customer service. Her name is Sally Sellers, our top performing sales person. Let's go downstairs to the sales floor and spend some time with her." As they prepared to leave the training room, a tall, slender redhead with a pleasant smile came out of the elevator. "Sally", Oscar said, "We were on our way to your work station." Sally said, "I knew you would be coming, but I wanted to come to the training room to talk to the trainees and to give my undivided attention. It is so busy down on the sales floor." Oscar said, "Well guys, grab a snack and let's take our seats. Sally is well worth listening to." Sally said to the group, "I'm sure most of you have bought a car before. As a sales person I have made it my business to make the process as painless as possible for my guests. I have discovered three secrets to success. As long as I stay focused on these I make big bucks and create raving fan customers. The three secrets are

1.   Desire to be the best.

2.   Finesse—people skills

3.   Product Knowledge

Sally said, "Being number one in sales in the 21st century demands that you have some quality customer service systems. I believe you have desire because you are here. Product knowledge is an elephant that you must eat one bite at a time. But today I want to focus on a system that will help you practice more finesse. Here is my threefold system and how it works." Sally went to the board and wrote: *A Threefold Customer Service System!*

Sally pulled out three rubber balls and said, "Heads up guys!" She shouted, "ATTITUDE," as she threw a ball to Joe. Then she yelled, "ART," and threw a ball to a young trainee that happened to be named Arthur. Then she looked around the room and saw a 6'5" trainee named Big John and said, "This one is BIG" and yelled "PROCESS" as she threw the third ball to John. "Customer service is an attitude, an art, and a process!"

The Threefold Customer Service System

- Art
- Attitude
- Process

Sally said, "The first part of the customer service system is **Attitude**. Your attitude is a trap or it is a freedom. In my studies of the behavioral sciences, I learned that people are not the creatures of circumstances; circumstances are the creatures of people. I like that because that means I CAN CREATE MY OWN ATTITUDE! Always remember that attitude is more important than facts, gifts or skills. It can make or break a business, a home, a family, or a church. Your Attitude is your mental posture or your way of thinking." Sally said, "Always remember, even if you have to read this everyday.

"Your Attitude Controls Your Altitude!"

Joe said, "This really sounds familiar." Sally said, "I know. George talked to you about attitude, didn't he?" Joe said, "He sure did."

Sally then continued, "The next thing you must know is that customer service is an **Art**—Service should be creative! Use your creative imagination to enhance the service experience. There is no 100%, only close and closer. Service is a continuous creative pursuit. **It's an art.** The Art of Rapport is a crucial skill in the Gospel of Customer Service. Customer service agents must understand the basics of body language to build rapport with customers."

Research shows that of our communication:

- 7% comes from the words we use

- 38% comes from our voice tonality (pitch and pace of words)

- 55% comes from our physiology (body) and posture

Sally then said, "To be effective in the Art of Rapport you must understand how to match and pace your customer in the areas of words, tone, and physiology. This increases the customer's comfort level. SERVICE IS AN ART!"

"Finally, in the big three, we must understand that customer service is A Process! Service is a **Process**—a process is a system. Finding the best way to do things is continuous. An effective process is the best way known to do a task. It brings order to the components of service. It leaves you free to concentrate on the finer things and add touches that make service come alive. It makes measuring progress possible, which is the key to continuous improvement. It facilitates consistency over a large and growing organization."

Sally then said to the group, "As a top performing sales consultant with the Southeast's fastest growing auto group, I have learned that to truly serve with excellence and go for the gold, you need to be Challenging Yourself to Be Extraordinary."

Sally said, "I love this quote: The difference between ordinary and extraordinary is that little extra. Extraordinary Service is the Key to More Customers, More Sales, and More Profits—BIG BUCKS! How many times have you been treated poorly by a business in the last 30 days? KAIZEN is the Japanese philosophy about how one approaches work: meaning continuous improvement (better, faster, more efficient ways of doing it). Challenge yourself to make improvements in your job and you will be motivated to achieve them. Kaizen will make you extraordinary!"

Sally said to the trainees, "Let's take a look at *12 Failure Systems* for dealerships. By the way, Oscar does an excellent job keeping us focused so that we don't fall into these."

1. Desired inventory is not in stock.

2. When you deliver no service or poor service after the sale.

3. Sales people who are poorly trained, uninformed, or distracted.

4. Red tape and bureaucratic processes.

5. Making customers wait to get into finance or to spend money.

6. Tricky pricing—phony numbers marked on vehicles.

7. Misleading advertising—bait and switch tactics.

8. Value is not commensurate to the price of the automobile.

9. The parts department with poor quality product and accessories.

10. Failing to stand behind vehicles or services.

11. The dealership with poor housekeeping, dirt, disorder, safety hazards.

12. Inconvenience: location, layout, parking.

Joe thought to himself, "She is a real disciple of Oscar. You can tell who she's been hanging around!"

Sally then said, "I don't need a crystal ball to give you this prophetic word. Here it is: OPERATE YOUR BUSINESS THIS WAY AND I WILL PREDICT YOUR FUTURE—FAILURE! Failure systems produce failure. These twelve, not handled properly, kills a business and sales success."

Sally said, "I have a gift for you. Here it is: **Good is the enemy of best!** One giant in business, who is also a personal friend, often uses the phrase *Best Practices*. In this concept, you look at what has and what has not worked in your industry (even borrowing from competitors). You simply eliminate the failure systems and adapt the success systems that give you the highest chance of success. You then ingrain them into the corporate culture, as a training program as "Best practices." Best practices are a form of success systems."

Sally said, "Let's now look at one of my favorite parts of the whole program. One of the major ways to cut down on upset customers is to understand **Training Ingrains Systems**. We must transform our information to add value to our customers by systematic training. Training ingrains systems into the corporate culture. Here are eight vital things to understand about training. I call it training for reigning! Catchy huh?" ☺

Training for Reigning

1. **Align your values with your vision!** Why am I doing this? Your work must have purpose and lead to a desired result. Begin with the end in mind.

2. **Learn to think strategically!** Tactical reactive work may not lead you to the desired end. A clearly defined mission or statement of goals is absolutely necessary to stay focused and reduce the clutter of everyday living and working

3. **Gather your resources!** No one has enough time, money, people or information. What do you need to accomplish your mission? Stay flexible.

4. **Manage your priorities every day!** If you are working on anything that does not lead to your ultimate vision in life, STOP. You are wasting resources and limiting your personal effectiveness.

5. **Measure your results.** Is your customer base full of Raving Fans or satisfied customers? ASK THEM.

6. **Take ownership of your work.** How can you be effective if you don't? Personal responsibility = ownership. The attitude of ownership is unique.

7. **Improve your ability to influence others**. Command and control is either dead or dying in today's work place. You move ahead by discussing, selling, influencing, inspiring or convincing. Learn to deal with others as partners in a collaborative relationship.

8. **No matter how well you do your job, improve on it everyday!** World class is doing it better today than yesterday and better than tomorrow. Sounds simple but recognizing the demand of our new economy is one thing. Resolving to do something to change it is another.

"Any business, organization or church that is not engaging in ongoing systematic training is not serious about customer service. Here at EXCELLENT WAY AUTOMOTIVE GROUP, we use this training room nearly every week of the year except the week after the holiday season. We have an administrative assistant that schedules classes and issues calendars constantly. Most car dealerships use the training room as a lunch room and usually have outdated training materials stacked in the corner next to the Eddie Murphy videos that the guys watch for laughs while waiting for customers. We are staunch believers of ongoing training. You could say we are religious about it!"—☺

O THANK HEAVEN FOR SALLY'S SEVEN

This is what I call **SALLY'S SEVEN**—they work!!!
Here are Seven Tips that make up a Success System of Extraordinary Service:

1. **Make Lasting First Impressions**—From the moment potential customers walk through the door or call on the phone, they are making a decision if they are going to do business with you or not. Greet the customer with enthusiasm and a smile; welcome them as you would a friend into your home.

2. **Ask the customer**—Ask them for suggestion on what you can do to improve your level of service. Ask them what other products or services would they like to see you carry in your store. Ask them for 3 reasons they do business with you. It will send a clear message to the customer that you value their feedback.

3. **Remember Special Dates**—When was the last time any company that you have done business with remembered a special, significant date in your life? Build a profile on each customer. Ask them to provide you with birthdates and anniversaries. In recognition of their anniversary as a customer, send them a gift or card from the business.

4. **Give Them Added Value**—The average business spends six times as much money attracting new customers as it does retaining existing ones. Invest in your existing customers: customer appreciation day, free gifts. Show them that you care!

5. **Show Appreciation**—When was the last time you received a thank you note or a heartfelt thank you for spending your hard earned money with a business? Look your customers in the eyes and say, "Thank you for doing business with me."

6. **Keep In Touch With Your Customers**—How often do you hear from the insurance agent that handles your insurance needs, or the real-estate agent that sold you a house, or the countless other businesses that have provided you a product or a service?

7. **Take Care of Your Customers**—Whether it's the person stocking shelves or the person behind the cash register, taking care of customers is everyone's job!

WHERE'S THE COMPLAINT DEPARTMENT???!!!!

Sally then said, "To discover what the customer wants, you must train yourself to welcome customer complaints. Most customer service reps run from and avoid complaints. But, the fact is, if you want to create customers that brag about your service, you must pay close attention to complaints. The numbers tell us that: 96% of unhappy customers that have a complaint won't complain (91% never return): for every complaint you get, there are 26 unhappy customers you don't hear from; the typical dissatisfied customer will tell eight to ten people; 70% of complaining customers will do business again if you make an effort to make them happy; 90—95% or more will do business with you again if you jump through hoops to make them happy! This goes up to 96-97% if you solve their problem on the spot! Listening, without interrupting, is about 60% of the solution."

Here is some of the best stuff I found that you could use in understanding customer complaints. **Apathy:** Some team members believe that their job is to shuffle paper and pound a computer keyboard. Our primary job should be to serve people—help people and offer good solutions. **Insolence:** Sometimes we are a bit too proficient in brushing people off with standard procedures. It let's us off the hook, or so it seems, but causes less than ideal customer service. **Curtness:** How many customers feel like they are an interruption to the customer service representative's day? **Patronization:** Treating the customer poorly is hardly a way to encourage repeat business, but it is the norm in many businesses. **Routine:** Team members who merely go through the motions are transparent to customers. **Runarounds:** Some customers get dizzy from being shifted from person to person.

Sally said, "I've developed a strategy I used, and still use, when dealing with a disappointed customer. Complaints are inevitable. Only responses are optional. Customer complaints are an opportunity."

Here is the complaint resolution strategy:

1. Hear it out completely.

2. Don't defend! Empathize—I understand how you feel. If I were in your situation, I would feel the same way.

3. Apologize—I'm sorry. Offer to resolve the problem immediately.

4. Make amends—Do something extra for the customer.

Sally then said enthusiastically, "All **great** customer service organizations understand this," as she pointed to a large poster on the back wall.

"There are only two things any customer buys. First, they buy solutions to problems. Customers generally don't buy tangible products—they buy solutions! They want products for the problems they solve. Second, they buy feelings. Customers want more than a product. They want to feel good about themselves. They also want to feel direct contact with you and your organization. In the final analysis, the success or failure of our organization depends on how many people we reward with those two things.

Now let's look into some reasons why customers get upset. Many businesses fail to understand that most customers get upset due to a lack of the company having a clearly defined service strategy. I know that some customers get upset because they may be angry at life in general. There may be little you can do for such persons except listen. Research reveals that many get upset legitimately due to an organization's lack of a clear strategy or not implementing the strategy they have on paper. The long and short of it is those customers believe that most mission statements are just wall plaques. Here are some factors that upset customers. You may bear the brunt of having associates who are inept coworkers, misrepresented things, don't have proper product knowledge, expectations aren't met, deliver less than you promise or someone else in your organization was either rude or indifferent.

Think back to the main reason why customers switch; not price, not product quality, but because of how they are treated. Customers have to wait. People hate to wait. We live in a fast paced world. Customers are often not taken seriously. If they have a complaint, they want to be noticed and to be acknowledged. Customers are sometimes embarrassed and act angry because they did something wrong. The key—always allow the customer to save face! The customer's integrity or honesty may have been challenged. Give the benefit of the doubt. Somebody from your organization may have argued with the customer. There is no such thing as a win/lose situation. If the customer loses, we all lose. Perhaps the customer is incensed because he or she has been given rules, procedures or policies that limit what you can do for them. And the beat goes on...Your attitude must be to help them all you can."

GET THE PHONE!

Sally said, "To be a real customer service pro you must work on your phone skills. From the moment you reach for the phone, use it as a powerful tool. Don't fall into the trap of being sloppy over the phone just because people can't see you. They can sense your concern, or lack of it. Make the telephone your ally, not your enemy! Remember, one customer served in an excellent manner can influence two hundred and fifty others to do business with you! This is the law of increase in motion! One customer abused in person or on the phone can influence as many or more not to do business with you. Since callers can't see you, your voice must feel welcoming. Enthusiasm, if genuine and warm, builds confidence. Limit your talking.

Irate callers often have a lot of pent up frustration. Listen to them patiently, and then they will be more likely to calm down and state real problems. Ask thoughtful questions. Probe so you can feel and verbalize his or her complaints, wants, needs, desires, and wishes. Repeat the problem in the caller's words. By doing this, you provide valuable feedback. By using words as close to the caller's own as possible, you show that you truly grasp the problem and its implications.

Concentrate on the caller's words and meaning. Give the customer your full attention. They can sense when you are distracted or bored. When they feel you are genuinely interested, they generally grow more amused. Offer encouragement. Say, "I understand what you are saying. I can see how you feel." Use word tracts. Say, "Exactly", "I understand what you are saying"; "I can see how you feel." **Always thank the person for calling."**

Oscar came in and beamed with a smile. He was so proud of Sally that tears welled up in his eyes. She had come to his dealership broke and broken hearted from a life of abuse. She was now truly a great one in customer service: a home-owner, a successful single mother of two teenage boys, and a productive part of society. Oscar said, "Sally you are my pride and joy! You are God's best!" Joe said, "You sure are free with compliments." Oscar replied, "Yes Joe. We have created a culture where we don't hold back legitimate compliments. Cheering each other on as we work together is the gift of the goose. It releases more energy, creativity, and enthusiasm." Joe's mind went back to the Canadian geese he had seen earlier, and thought, "ah ha!"

Let's take a fifteen-minute break and I'll meet you upstairs to wrap up the day and the training program.

GOING THE EXTRA MILE

Oscar said, "We are now going to deal with the strategies that will make you a customer service legend. Jesus called it going the extra mile. I like to call it **deliver more than you promise**! Don't drive promise down; drive delivery up! Customer Expectations: Meet first; exceed second. If you fall short of what you said you would do, the customer feels cheated.

Here is a real life example of a poor system. I was at a car dealership recently getting my wife's car serviced. It took the service writer about thirty minutes to complete the write-up for me to sign so that I could leave. Granted, my wife did have a list of about five items. The real problem was in a flawed service system. The service writers were required to go out and inspect the cars coming in, write up the service order, and ANSWER THE INCOMING CALLS. The guy received about three calls, wrote up their service orders over the phone, while several paying customers stood impatiently in line. Requiring that they answer the phone is a part of a faulty service system. The man was a pleasant fellow that did not have a clue of the negative impact this was having. I left and told a friend if they were not the only manufacturer of the product in the area, I definitely wouldn't go back...WE MUST ANALYZE SYSTEMS TO MAKE SURE THEY ARE Customer FRIENDLY!"

Oscar asked if the trainees had learned anything. They said, "More than we ever imagined in an orientation for a car dealership." Joe said, "My neighbor went to work for a local family owned dealership and he said the training program was a stack of out-dated videos to take home and watch. This is first class!"

"Here is a critical success factor in customer service. **All good customer service is the result of effective systems.** Create happy customers by building systems that help you to look after the customer's needs whenever possible. This whole three day training program is about a system. To drive the point home, you could say the three spiritual principles of the book make a system of service. Let's look at them again:

1. **A Meaningful Service Vision**

2. **Customer Oriented People**

3. **Customer Friendly Systems**

You must have systems. Become a fanatic of systems. Systems are what allow you to guarantee delivery, not just smiling and saying, "Have a nice day." A training program should ingrain the systems into the soul of the department. After training, you must establish your Performance Standards, which are the foundation of Customer Service Excellence."

- Train people to follow systems.

- Systems are worth not a dime if people aren't trained to follow them.

- **Deliver it time after time, without fail, in sync with the system.**

Oscar flipped the page on his flip chart and said, "Check this out!"

> *At the core of every great customer service organization is a package of systems and a training program to inculcate those programs into the soul of the company.*
> **—Ken Blanchard, Raving Fans**

With a rule, the emphasis is simply a procedure or policy and not the result. However, you must have rules. At a gas station, not smoking within ten feet of the pump is a good rule. Systems help to deliver service. Systems are predetermined ways to achieve results. The emphasis has to be on achieving the result and not the system for the system's sake.

Plays in sports are a type of system. The systems set guidelines, but sometimes you must enhance the play to score. The purpose for systems is to ensure consistency, not to create robots. Rules do that. Systems give you a floor, not a ceiling. Systems allow you to deliver a standard of performance consistently. Systems bring order!

You can't reduce great service to systems alone but they are extremely important in the Gospel of Customer Service. A lot of companies have systems to extract cash from the customer's pocket, but I'm talking about excellent service, meeting needs! Customers have needs beyond the company's product. People need to feel they belong to a group. People need to feel they are important. The Gospel of Customer Service must become a part of the company's culture...not a flavor of the month.

The Apostle of Customer Service now said, "When you get to the sum of customer service, it's really all about caring! If I could sum it all up, I would say the Gospel of Customer Service is **Caring!"**

Extraordinary customer service is always a result of efficient systems. Excellent customer service will be the key factor not only in surviving, but also in prospering during the coming times of accelerated competition. In fact, customer care will soon become the business of businesses not just for your organization, but for everyone.

What is Customer Care? A sharp, clearly defined center of interest in delivering Ideal Customer Service! Focusing on what customers need and want. Remember, the only reason for being and staying in business is *customers*.

Summary of Spiritual Principle #3
Customer Friendly Systems

- Systems must be customer friendly
- Systems help you deliver more than you promise
- Delivery is where the rubber meets the road
- Systems are vital
- Systems—not rules

Oscar concluded, "It has been great sharing these concepts with you all. I hope we have shared something that will help you go out and make a difference, making the world a better place.

I will leave you with my final point. Always do more than what is expected of you. Always go the extra mile. If you do that, customers will remember you and come back. By the way, remember to fill out the evaluation form at the very end of the customer service training. At EXCELLENT WAY, we believe that feedback is the breakfast of champions!

Now let's all stand and say after me "IT'S A GREAT DAY AT EXCELLENT WAY!" The group enthusiastically did and Oscar gave them a big God Bless you all!

Joe Simple came up to thank Oscar for the life changing training and asked a question he had been wanting to ask ever since he met Oscar, but for professional reasons he hadn't. "Oscar, do you mind if I ask where you attend to Church?" Oscar said, "No, not at all. I attend Creative Concepts Faith Centre in Suwanee, Georgia, a suburb of Atlanta. CCFC is a Bible teaching non-denominational church. The vision statement is sharing a message of positive faith, helping humanity find purpose and significance." Joe thought to himself, "Interesting. Reminds me of Zack's type of Church. These new-style Churches seem to be the bomb today." Oscar interrupted his thoughts and said, "Joe I'll give you a map." Oscar gave Joe the address and service times.

12

THANK GOD IT'S SUNDAY!

◆

Again...

On the following Sunday, Joe drove into the parking lot of Creative Concepts to be met by a friendly parking lot attendant that opened the door of his BMW. "Good morning," the young man said cheerfully. Joe said, "Thanks" and went into the main auditorium. He thought, "Everyone here is so nice. It reminds me of the customer service at EXCELLENT WAY." After the praise and worship, Joe's jaw nearly hit the floor when the announcements were made and the assistant pastor said, "We will now have the Word for today from the pastor." Joe thought, "No! It can't be!" As Oscar came to the platform he waved and said, "Good Morning congregation. Let's open our Bibles today to Deuteronomy 8: 18...but before we read, let's all make our positive affirmation and shout, **"THANK GOD IT'S SUNDAY!"** Joe was blown away, and thought, "This is amazing. He did not tell me he was the pastor of a church during the training, this is incredible." After the powerful sermon on the Good News of Answering the Call to Wealth by Serving Others, Oscar gave an invitation for people to become believers. Joe thought, "I have heard enough. This is real. The gospel is not just for Sunday. It's for everyday." Joe said to himself, "True faith is about serving God through serving people everyday, in every possible way."

After Church, as Oscar was greeting the first time guests as they left, Joe walked up to him with a beaming smile. "You are too much! Why didn't you tell me you were the minister when you invited me to Church? Man you are good!" Oscar smiled real big, gave Joe a big hug and said, "God Alone is good! Welcome to the Family of customer service Joe! But Joe, I hope that through this experience you have seen the moral of the story." Joe said, "Yes I have." Oscar asked, "What is it?" Joe replied, "The Gospel of Customer Service is not just for Sunday. It's about people serving people in every way, every day! Thank God It's Sunday!"

Oscar concluded by saying, "Remember, the Gospel according to Nordstrom—*this is what we are here for, to serve and to be kind.*"

OSCAR'S CONFESSION!

Before you close this book and put it in shelf-land, I want you to know that this parable is based on a true story. I'm Oscar Bernard Smalls. In elementary school kids called me the Oscar Meyer wiener boy. I hated it. So, I encourage everyone to call me by my middle name, which is Bernard, with my mother's agreement. In college I had to set professors straight in each new class. Every once in a while someone still looks at my legal name at DMV and calls out that wonderful name.

Well, now I operate as corporate trainer for one of the greatest automobile dealerships and automotive groups in the history of the world. The dealership is Toyota Mall of Georgia. With the excellent customer service and marketing concepts of our fearless leader and owner John Williams, we made history by winning all ten of Toyota's Distinguished Service Excellence Awards in the first full year of business. This is the first and only time this has been done in Toyota Motor Corporation, in the seventy-four year history of producing quality vehicles. I am a believer and an ordained minister.

My corporate pulpit has been the training room at Toyota Mall where people come weekly seeking a career opportunity that will better their financial lives and the lives of their loved ones. **I don't preach religion; I preach service.** I've had many Joe's in my customer service classes that have spanned approximately three years. Several have ended up becoming a part of our local church. I even performed the marriage ceremony for one of the men that attended the first training class I did for the organization. I even get a little preachy sometimes. In several sales meetings, people have responded with an AMEN! I can assure you that the Gospel of Customer Service, or Spiritual Pragmatism, is the Gospel Truth and it works! I've proven it! Been there, done that, bought the tee shirt! It's Excellent!

The good news is The Gospel of Customer Service is not just for Sunday. In fact, it's not a religious thing but it is a *spiritual thing*. As spiritual beings deep down within us we all know it. It's for everyday people, everyday! It's about simply finding a hurt and healing it, finding a need and meeting it. Wouldn't that make the world a better place? We don't need more religion; we need more people that will go about doing good by serving humanity!

PASS IT ON!!!

T.G.I.S.-day,

Bernard (Oscar—☺)

BIBLIOGRAPHY

Anderson, Kristin and Ron Zemke. *Delivering Knock Your Socks Off Service.* Amacom. New York. 1998

Blanchard, Kenneth H. and Sheldon Bowles. *Raving Fans—A revolutionary approach to customer service.* Jossey Bass. New York. 1993

Blanchard, Kenneth H. and Sheldon Bowles. *Gung Ho!* Morrow and Williams Company. New York. 1997

Blanchard, Kenneth H. and Sheldon Bowles. *Big Bucks! How to Make Serious Money for You and Your Company.* Harper Collins Publishers. New York. 2000

Blanchard, Kenneth H. and Jesse stoner. Full Steam Ahead—Unleashing The Power of Vision in Your Company and Your Life. Berrett-Koehler Publishers. San Francisco. 2003

Carlzon, Jan and Tom Peters. *Moments of Truth.* Harper Collins Publishing. New York. 1989

Covey, Stephen R. *The Seven Habits of Highly Effective People—Powerful Lessons in Personal Change. Fireside*—Simon & Schuster. New York. 1990

Daniels, Peter J. *How to Reach Your Life Goals.* The House of Tabor. Australia. 1985

Peters, Thomas and Robert H. Waterman, Jr. In Search of Excellence—*Lessons from America's Best-Run Companies.* Warner Brothers. New York. 1992

Sanders, Elizabeth A. Fabled Service—*Ordinary Acts/Extraordinary Outcomes.* Jossey-Bass. New York. 1995

Wiersema, Fred. Customer Service—*Outstanding Results*. DIANE Publishing Company. Pennsylvania. 2000

Ziglar, Zig. Secrets of Closing the Sale. Berkley Publishing Group. New York. 1985

ABOUT THE AUTHOR

Bernard Smalls is a corporate trainer and a consulting resource with The Ken Blanchard Companies. He lives in Atlanta, Georgia and holds a Bachelor of Philosophy in Theology Degree. Bernard helped put Toyota Mall on the map by winning every service excellence award (ten) in Toyota's History.

For seminars or keynote speeches contact:

O. Bernard Smalls
Founding Concepts Training & Development
P.O. Box 1359
Suwanee, Georgia 30024
678. 482.8411

www.foundingconcepts.com

0-595-29606-8